ONE HEALTH

ONE HEALTH

A Sociological Perspective

BY

ANTONIO MATURO

University of Bologna, Italy

emerald PUBLISHING

United Kingdom – North America – Japan – India
Malaysia – China

Emerald Publishing Limited
Howard House, Wagon Lane, Bingley BD16 1WA, UK

First edition 2026

British Library Cataloguing in Publication Data
A catalogue record for this book is available from the British Library

ISBN: 978-1-83708-391-6 (Print)
ISBN: 978-1-83708-388-6 (Online)
ISBN: 978-1-83708-390-9 (Epub)

INVESTOR IN PEOPLE

CONTENTS

INTRODUCTION

This is not a sociological book on One Health (OH). It does not offer a detailed, precise sociological analysis of OH. What I aim to do here is to show how sociology can be useful for the development of the OH approach. Sociology can be used both to reflect theoretically on OH and to support the OH approach in situations of intervention and empirical research. This book is, therefore, primarily aimed at people who do not have a solid background in sociology, and readers will not find reflections on OH on every page. Each page does, however, contain notions, concepts, and techniques that (I hope) can be applied, more or less directly, to OH.

The OH approach is based on the idea that there is a strong interdependence between animal, human, and environmental health. Health is one, and no single dimension takes precedence over another. Therefore, OH is a *naturally* interdisciplinary approach. It may be useful for researchers working on OH, such as veterinarians, doctors, environmental scientists, biologists, and other social scientists, to be aware of the role that sociology, specifically health sociology, can play in OH. Obviously, for the curious sociologists seeking to approach OH, my reflections may make the start of their journey a little smoother and more familiar.

As several sources have indicated, the concept of OH originated in the field of veterinary science. It is, therefore, no surprise that most reflections on OH focus on aspects related to zoonoses, spillover, and, in general, infectious diseases transmitted from animals to humans (and vice versa).

After all, according to the *World Organisation for Animal Health*, 60% of human infectious diseases are zoonotic and 75% of emerging human infectious diseases originate from other animal species.

There are also numerous studies on policies regarding the implementation of OH in institutional settings, but scant consideration is given to the social sciences, specifically sociology, and health sociology (my discipline, if I may say so) in particular. Obviously, this is partly our own fault, as we are rather picky and tend to remain somewhat on the sidelines.

If we take a look at *One Health*,[1] a prestigious journal with a high CiteScore and impact factor, the website effectively states that it welcomes articles on the following topics: "virology, bacteriology, parasitology, mycology, vectors and vector-borne diseases, co-infections and co-morbidities, disease spatial surveillance, modelling, tropical health, discovery, ecosystem health, public health."

Clearly, there is nothing wrong with this, especially since the journal is promoted by *the International Federation for Tropical Medicine*. With great intellectual honesty, it is best to stay within one's area of expertise (which the journal does excellently). Another journal of absolute scientific rigor, the *International Journal of One Health* – which, according to its website, has an article acceptance rate of 28% – has the scientific objective of publishing: "high quality and novelty papers focusing on One Health: Topics include One Health, Antimicrobial resistance, Zoonoses, Foodborne pathogens and diseases, Bioterrorism, Ethnomedicine, Climate change."[2] There is not a significant presence of social sciences here either, apart from ethnomedicine perhaps (which, let's face it, has more to do with anthropology than with sociology).

Incidentally, those involved in sociology in the field of health already suffer from inferiority complexes due to medical snobbery. But let's leave out the psychoanalysis and turn directly to the content of this work. The book is divided into six chapters, plus a final chapter.

In the first chapter, *More than One Health*, I highlight the differences and similarities between One Health and other institutional and non-institutional concepts of health. In particular, I focus on the differences between OH approaches and those based on Global Health and Planetary Health. I also describe and analyze the main elements of theories related to post-colonial health, focusing on its aspects of institutional criticism. I mention the fact that sociology can play a critical role in OH.

In the second chapter, *Living in the Risk Society*, I introduce two sociological concepts that may be of some importance in OH: risk and trust. In sociology, there has long been talk of the risk society. The term describes multiple dimensions, including those related to globalization and the interdependence of health risks. I also show how risks spread not only in space, but also in time and at social level, and that there is a relationship with social inequality and vulnerability. With regard to trust, I review the arguments on the crisis of social trust in science, with a particular focus on vaccine hesitancy.

In the third chapter, *Prospects for the Future: Theories and Methodologies to Prevent Another Pandemic*, I emphasize the central role of OH in predicting potential ecological and pandemic disasters. I dwell again on the relationship between science and society, showing that there are many cases of "undone science," that is, scientific areas that have not been developed for political and economic reasons, with the result that they simply do not exist in reality. This phenomenon is explained using the sociology of ignorance: a fruitful theoretical apparatus that demonstrates how "actively" ignoring certain problems allows us to influence political decisions that perpetuate social inequalities and ecological imbalances. This aspect is linked to the importance of foresight today: our knowledge (or lack of knowledge) of the present also influences our preparedness for environmental and health risks. In addition to focusing on the difference between foresight and forecasting, I propose and analyze a number of sociological methodologies for constructing future scenarios.

In the fourth chapter, *Sociological Theories for One Health*, I analyze the practical use of sociological theories in OH. First and foremost, I show the importance for OH of sociological theories that relate social inequality to people's health. For example, we know that people of low socioeconomic status are highly vulnerable to the consequences of urbanization and natural disasters. On the other hand, the theory of the social construction of reality can help us understand why so many people are drawn to extravagant and dangerous ideas about vaccines, because this theory seeks to understand how beliefs and social representations arise. Midway between critical theory and the theory of the social construction of reality we find studies on social stigma. On this point, the chapter offers the example of Chagas disease (American Trypanosomiasis). Finally, thanks to Gregory Bateson's theory of the "ecology of mind," I provide a set of theoretical concepts useful for understanding the epistemology of OH.

In the fifth chapter, *One Health: Some Theories of Justice*, I explore the ethical complexity of OH. A multidimensional and interdependent approach such as OH requires different levels of ethical analysis. The discussion begins with environmental justice, which focuses on the link between social inequalities, vulnerabilities, and health disparities. I go on to mention the sustainability principle, which underpins intergenerational justice, that is, the responsibility of present generations for generations yet to come. I obviously take interspecies justice into consideration, given that OH also deals with non-human animals.

In the sixth chapter, *One Health and Social Participation: The Role of Transdisciplinarity, Multisectorality, and Knowledge Integration*, I explore the OH approach through the lens of social participation, with a specific focus on transdisciplinarity, multisectorality, and knowledge integration. Central to this discussion is understanding that active, diverse involvement on the part of social actors is essential to address the complex challenges characterizing the interconnection between human, animal, and environmental health. The chapter highlights how a transdisciplinary and multisectoral approach, supported by methodologies such as co-creation and design thinking, can overcome traditional "silos" and foster more democratic and inclusive governance in the field of OH.

As the reader can observe, I do not reach Conclusions, but rather *Unclusions*, in the sense that the discussion on the contribution of sociology to OH is by no means concluded with my analyses (which are partial and can be improved). There may of course be sociologists who see the contribution of sociology differently. An environmental sociologist would probably have developed the aspects related to environmental justice in greater depth. A political sociologist would have emphasized the aspects of governance, including international governance, provided for by the different institutional definitions of OH. Since my passion is health sociology, I have my own inclinations.

In the final chapter, I will be making two proposals. The first concerns the relationship between OH and sociological knowledge. I will propose three characteristics of OH that in my opinion make this perspective entirely unique and original, when viewed through a sociological framework. The second proposal concerns the areas of OH in which the sociological approach can be used at an operational level: critical analysis, methodology for social participation, methodology applied to future studies. Both proposals are largely unrelated to the sociology of health (with the exception of the discussion on the exposome).

I was prompted to write this book by my involvement with the Self Steering Committee on OH at the University of Bologna. The driving force behind the Committee is Alessandra Scagliarini, who introduced me to the main concepts of OH from the perspective of a veterinary science lecturer. It was a very useful exercise in shifting my perspective. The other two members of the Committee, Alessandra De Cesare, and Viviana Cocchi also suggested several topics. In general, the One Health group of Una Europa (a consortium of 11 European universities) has been a source of numerous stimuli. I must at least mention Bruno González Zorn, our current chair of One Health/Una Europa, and the indefatigable Paula Martín of the Complutense University of Madrid. I discussed the topic of sustainability with Thilo Kroll of University College Dublin one fine October afternoon at the Complutense University of Madrid, where a Una Europa meeting was taking place. I would also like to thank Robbert Boudewijns (KU Leuven), Lisa Boden (University of Edinburgh), Gerardine Doyle (University College

Dublin), Cecile Falies (Université Paris 1 Panthéon-Sorbonne), Sarah Green (University of Helsinki), Annamari Heikinheimo (University of Helsinki), Thomas Lutz (Universität Zürich), Topi Tanskanen (University of Helsinki), and Juergen Zentek (Freie Universität Berlin) for our informal but fruitful conversations.

I must sincerely thank Annalisa Plava, Marta Gibin, Riccardo Pronzato, and Asia Ferroni for their discussions and practical help in writing this book. Veronica Moretti and Elisa Castellaccio were unwitting sources of inspiration for many of the topics discussed here.

I find dealing with colleagues from other disciplines complicated. With age, I have developed a series of comfortable prejudices and fixed ideas that simplify my life or, to borrow a term from sociology, reduce complexity. Having to deal with approaches and cognitive frames that are far removed from sociology has forced me to reactivate my thinking and review many of my beliefs. It has been arduous, but I have learned many things, which has made me feel more flexible and less old, so it has all been worthwhile. Explaining sociology to people from other disciplines has also been a challenging exercise, and I am not sure if I have always been successful. This last point allows me to emphasize once again that this volume is intended to be both an innovative contribution and a work designed to popularize sociology. I have done my best to write clearly and readably (no easy task for someone who is both a sociologist and Italian). I have also reduced the bibliographical references to a minimum so as not to weigh down the reading experience. I even disobeyed ChatGPT, which had generated a totally different index for this book.

...but to be completely honest, the *urgent* impulse to write this book came to me one evening in November 2024, during a conference on One Health held in Italy. I had the following conversation with a foreign colleague from Northern Europe, a veterinarian with no involvement in the social sciences:

> *Veterinarian: "We would like to collaborate with sociologists, but we really don't understand them."*
>
> *Me: "I get that sociologists' books are sometimes written with somewhat exotic expressions and convoluted arguments, but often when you talk to people, you come to understand them."*
>
> *Vet: "No, no, we had a meeting with sociologist colleagues from our university, but we were on totally different levels. I felt stupid. I didn't understand their words..."*

I poured two glasses of red wine (Sangiovese), one for myself and one for my colleague:

> *Me: "Yes, even I sometimes struggle to understand my colleagues when they write, and it used to be even worse: it was once considered chic in Italy to write books that were incomprehensible."*
>
> *Vet: "It would be great to have a book that could give us a smattering of knowledge about the relationship between sociology and One Health."*
>
> *Me: "The die is cast. The famous phrase was pronounced not far from here, by the way. Cheers, or rather 'to your health!'* No, *to One Health!"*
>
> *Vet: "Wine Health:)"*

NOTES

1. https://www.sciencedirect.com/journal/one-health/about/aims-and-scope, accessed 8 December 2025.

2. https://onehealthjournal.org/about.php, accessed 8 December 2025.

1

MORE THAN ONE HEALTH

ABSTRACT

This chapter will be exploring the evolution of the One Health concept and how it relates to global health and planetary health. Over the years, this approach has gained strong institutional recognition, culminating in the creation of coordinating bodies at international level and the integration of its principles into policy agendas. However, One Health is not exempt from criticism. Often noted is an excessive focus on emerging zoonotic diseases and insufficient consideration of environmental dimensions and complex social dynamics that influence health. In the face of these limitations, the concept of planetary health emerges as an attempt to broaden the view, seeking to include the challenges posed by climate change, biodiversity loss, and the growing anthropogenic pressure on ecosystems. Parallel to this, global health contains a strong political dimension that can guide different policies and interventions related to human, animal, and environmental health. These three approaches should, therefore, be considered under a wider integrative perspective. Last but not least, the post-colonial reflections on health may shed light on power dynamics and on how social institutions and their modes of organization are shaped to confirm and legitimize the status quo.

Keywords: One Health; planetary health; global health; post-colonial health; zoonotic diseases; Critical approach

INTRODUCTION

In the increasingly interconnected and complex landscape of health, the traditional view that considers human, animal, and environmental health separately is proving inadequate. This chapter will be exploring the evolution of the "One Health" concept and how it relates to global health and planetary health. As we shall see, One Health is not a recent invention. It is rooted in an understanding of the interdependence between humans, animals, and ecosystems that goes back thousands of years and has been rediscovered and valued in recent times, partly thanks to the pioneering work of figures such as Rudolf Virchow. Over the years, this approach has gained strong institutional recognition, culminating in the creation of coordinating bodies at international level and the integration of its principles into policy agendas. However, as we shall also see in other parts of the book, One Health is not exempt from criticism. Often noted is an excessive focus on emerging zoonotic diseases and insufficient consideration of environmental dimensions and complex social dynamics that influence health. In the face of these limitations, the concept of planetary health emerges as an attempt to broaden the view, seeking to include the challenges posed by climate change, biodiversity loss, and the growing anthropogenic pressure on ecosystems. But how are these three approaches related? Should we consider them as separate responses to different problems, or should we aspire to a conceptual convergence that integrates the insights of One Health and planetary health within a broader framework of global health? This chapter will explore these questions, analyzing the opportunities and challenges raised by an integrated, transdisciplinary approach that promotes the health and well-being of all species, while respecting the limits of our planet. We will be exploring these questions from a sociological perspective.

WHAT IS ONE HEALTH?

The One Health approach is neither a recent discovery nor a recent invention. The idea of the interdependence between micro and macro, between Man and the cosmos, or between the human, animal, and natural kingdoms goes back a very long way. Today, this way of conceiving reality has obtained strong institutional recognition, so, the OH approach has not so much been invented as acknowledged and named. To put it clearly:

> *the One Health field has grown – and we recognize that in many ways the knowledge and terminology evolved back to what the*

indigenous peoples from across the world have been living and practicing for over 10,000 years. (Pettan-Brewer et al., 2024, p. 3)

Before describing how One Health has been recognized institutionally and then proposing a definition of One Health, I would like to recall that it was the German physician Rudolf Virchow (1821–1902) who coined the term "zoonosis," in the 19th century. Moreover, he also proclaimed,

there is no scientific barrier, nor should there be, between veterinary medicine and human medicine; the experience of one must be utilized for the development of the other. (Quoted in Sundberg & Schofield, 2009, p.1530)

It is only in recent times that OH has been formalized and internationally recognized. The first event it is important to mention is the conference entitled *One World, One Health: Building Interdisciplinary Bridges to Health in a Globalized World,* held in 2004 at the Rockefeller University in New York and coordinated by the Wildlife Conservation Society. At this conference, a group of experts led by Robert A. Cook and Steven A. Osofsky published a concluding synthesis containing 12 recommendations, labeled by the document's authors as the "Manhattan Principles".[1]

In 2008, the three major international organizations charged with animal health and human health – the UN Food and Agriculture Organization (FAO), the World Organisation for Animal Health (OIE), and the World Health Organization (WHO) – collaborated with the United Nations Children's Fund, the UN System for Influenza Coordinator, and the World Bank, to develop a joint strategic framework in response to the evolving risk of emerging and re-emerging infectious diseases. The document communicating this framework is titled: *Contributing to One World, One Health – A Strategic Framework for Reducing Risks of Infectious Diseases at the Animal–Human–Ecosystems Interface*. As page 6 of the document reads:

The overall objective of the Strategic Framework represents an international public good. Its achievement will involve the strengthening of existing animal and public health surveillance, response, prevention and preparedness systems at the country, regional and international levels. (FAO, OIE, WHO, Un System Influenza Coordination, UNICEF, THE WORLD BANK, 2008, p. 6)

After all, it is a known fact that around 70% of the emerging infectious diseases that have affected humans in the last 20 years are of animal origin, that is, they are zoonoses (Favretto & Balduzzi, 2023). These diseases can be transmitted from animals to humans through various routes, such as contact, food, stings from vector insects, or even bites. The major think tanks were already aware of the growing threat posed by zoonoses. As is also emphasized in the following pages, the increase in zoonoses is due to the progressive anthropization of the environment, so the growth of infectious diseases is ultimately caused by humans.

On February 17, 2021, during an opening address at an assembly held in the presence of other Tripartite organizations (Food and Agriculture Organization of the United Nations and WOAH, the World Organization of Animal Health, which at the time was named Office International des Epizootiees OIE), the Director-General of the World Health Organization, Tedros A. Ghebreyesus, stated that "the COVID-19 pandemic is a powerful demonstration that the health of humans, animals and eco-systems is intimately linked."

While OH may have seemed to many citizens as "simply a concept" in the past, Ghebreyesus continued,

> *it is no longer, – as it is now clear to everyone that – we can only prevent future pandemics with an integrated One Health approach to public health, animal health and the environment we share. (Ghebreyesus, 2021)*

Following a proposal made by the French and German Ministers for Foreign Affairs at the November 2020 Paris Peace Forum, four global partners (the tripartite organizations plus the United Nations Environment Programme UNEP, now the Quadripartite) in May 2021 established the interdisciplinary One Health High-Level Expert Panel (OHHLEP) to enhance their cross-sectoral collaboration. The creation of OHHLEP represents recognition of the urgency and complexities surrounding One Health and the intent to take this concept forward into policies (Favretto & Balduzzi, 2023). Based on the numerous academic and institutional definitions of OH, the OHHLEP came up with its own definition, which attempted to summarize the previous ones.

> *One Health is an integrated, unifying approach that aims to sustainably balance and optimize the health of people, animals, and ecosystems. It recognizes that the health of humans, domestic and wild animals, plants, and the wider environment (including ecosystems) are closely linked and interdependent.*
>
> *The approach mobilizes multiple sectors, disciplines and communities at varying levels of society to work together to foster well-being and tackle threats to health and ecosystems, while*

> *addressing the collective need for healthy food, water, energy, and air, taking action on climate change and contributing to sustainable development.*[2]

As can be seen in Fig. 1, the scope of OH's research and intervention is immense. It requires the coordination, at several levels, of extremely heterogeneous actors and competencies. Furthermore,

> *One Health, initially focused mostly on zoonotic diseases, has evolved in recent decades to include many other complex issues, such as antimicrobial resistance, re-emerging infectious and chronic non-infectious diseases, environmental contamination, climate change, food safety/security, loss of biodiversity, economic sustainability, social-ecological systems, traditional indigenous knowledge, ocean health, etc., requiring the adoption of a more transdisciplinary approach and multi-disciplinary competencies. (Pettan-Brewer et al., 2024, p. 2)*

Perhaps an OH approach may never be completely faithful to the definition of the OHHLEP, given how extensive the latter is. However, the right idea might be to start from the core of the definition and then focus, at a contingent and contextual level, on the contents and dimensions of OH specifically entailed by the object of research/intervention. In my view, the core of the OH definition is the recognition of interdependence.

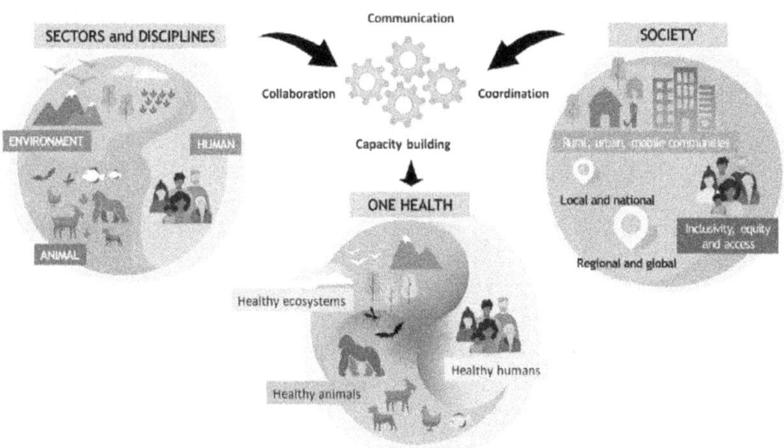

Fig. 1. One Health High-level Expert Panel (Adisasmito et al., 2022).

ONE HEALTH AND GLOBAL HEALTH

To understand how OH and the concept of global health are related and how they differ, we must first establish what global health is. And this is where the difficulties begin to arise. In the words of the renowned anthropologist Arthur Kleinman:

> *Global health, many would agree, is more a bunch of problems than a discipline. (Kleinman, 2010, p. 1518)*

Kleinman is not alone in expressing such misgivings. For Koplan et al., for example, the definition of global health:

> *varies greatly and is often little more than a rephrasing of a common definition of public health or a politically correct updating of international health. (Koplan et al., 2009, p. 1993)*

It is, therefore, worth taking a moment to define "public health" and "international health." For public health, the most familiar definition dates back more than a century and was provided by Charles-Edward Amory Winslow. Winslow was an important figure in the foundation of public health. In 1915, Professor Winslow founded the Yale Department of Public Health. He was professor and chairman of the Department until he retired in 1945:

> *Public health is the science and art of preventing disease, prolonging life and promoting physical health and efficacy through organized community efforts for the sanitation of the environment, the control of communicable infections, the education of the individual in personal hygiene, the organization of medical and nursing services for the early diagnosis and preventive treatment of disease, and the development of social machinery which will ensure every individual in the community a standard of living adequate for the maintenance of health; so organizing these benefits in such a fashion as to enable every citizen to realize his birthright and longevity. (Winslow, 1920, p. 30)*

Koplan et al. (2009, p. 1993) summarized the orientations of public health into four principles:

1. decision-making based on data and evidence (vital statistics, surveillance and outbreak investigations, laboratory science);
2. a focus on populations rather than individuals;
3. a goal of social justice and equity;
4. an emphasis on prevention rather than curative care.

Today, we probably take the existence of public health for granted, at least in countries that can implement welfare policies. However, when we take a closer look, we can see that each of those four principles has encountered problems in recent times. With regard to the first principle, COVID-19 has unleashed a number of anti-scientific forces that now enjoy a high reputation even in institutional circles; with regard to the second and fourth principles, the gradual spread of neo-liberal policies in health care has increasingly pushed for curative interventions on the individual, rather than public investment for the benefit of society as a whole; with regard to equity, this is certainly problematic in an environment increasingly dominated by profit, and in which the scientific approach is increasingly devalued. In 1920, Winslow wrote that:

> *In the past a sharp line was drawn between the measures taken by public health authorities to check the spread of epidemic disease and the daily routine of the practitioner in the treatment of the individual case. The first was public health, the second private medicine. With the passing of every year it becomes harder to draw such a sharp line, more difficult to say where public health should end and private medicine begin. (Winslow, 1920, p. 27)*

Today, this line is not only increasingly blurred, but has also shifted – higher or lower, depending on the observation point – and the area of public health has shrunk, while the area of private medicine has expanded enormously. The only difference is that private practitioners are increasingly being replaced by the Health Industrial Complex.

As for international health, the other "leg" of global health, we could get away with quite a simple definition. According to Merson et al., international health is nothing other than:

> *the application of the principles of public health to problems and challenges that affect low and middle-income countries and to the complex array of global and local forces that influence them. (Merson et al., 2006, p. 14)*

In the past, international health, as a field of study, has also dealt with the health policies of large international organizations. It has focused above all on health activities between governments or people from two or more nations, thus including WHO disease control programs, clinical services provided by medical missions and corporations, overseas research by universities, and populations and nutrition activities associated with health programs (Bryant & Velji, 2011).

To put it bluntly, we could say that the "leg" of public health provides the depth of intervention to global health, while the "leg" of international health provides the extent of intervention to global health (if you'll excuse the anthropocentric metaphor) (See Fig. 2).

Broadly speaking, global health as a term can be referred to

> *those health issues which transcend national boundaries and governments and call for actions on the global forces and global flows that determine the health of people. (Kickbush, 2006, p. 561)*

More specifically, it can be seen as:

> *an area for study, research, and practice that places a priority on improving health and achieving equity in health for all people worldwide. It emphasizes transnational health issues, determinants, and solutions; considers innovative ways to address those challenges, and promotes interdisciplinary collaboration (Koplan et al., 2009, 1993).*

Table 1, summarized from Koplan et al. (2009), effectively describes the comparison between these three perspectives, which are different, but interconnected, with several points of overlap.

How can we characterize the relationship between global health and One Health at this point?

The OH and global approaches have differences and similarities, yet they can play a complementary and synergetic role in health promotion and the improvement of health outcomes.

Global health takes a broad perspective, addressing health issues that affect humanity worldwide, including infectious diseases, social determinants, health systems, and inequalities.

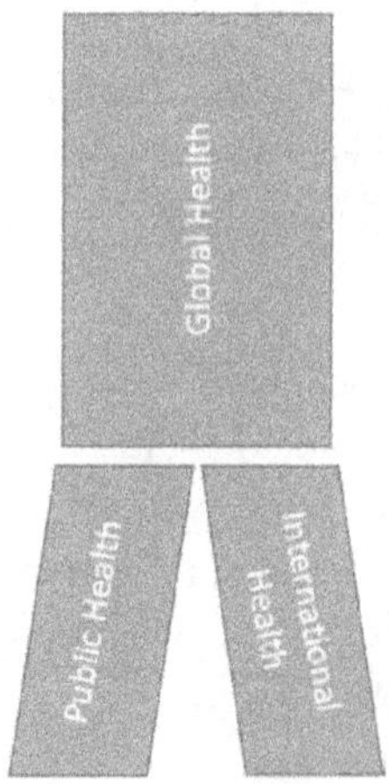

Fig. 2. The Two "Legs" of Global Health.

Table 1. Global Health, International Health, and Public Health.

	Global Health	International Health	Public Health
Geographical reach	Focuses on issues that directly or indirectly affect health but that can transcend national boundaries	Focuses on health issues of countries other than one's own, especially those of low-income and middle-income	Focuses on issues that affect the health of a population of a particular community or country
Level of cooperation	Development and implementation of solutions often requires global cooperation	Development and implementation of solutions usually requires binational cooperation	Development and implementation of solutions does not usually requires global cooperation
Individuals or populations	Embraces both prevention in populations and clinical care of individuals	Embraces both prevention in populations and clinical care of individuals	Mainly focuses on prevention programs for populations
Access to health	Health equity among nations and for all people is a major objective	Seeks to help people of other nations	Health equity within a nation or community is a major objective
Range of disciplines	Highly interdisciplinary and multidisciplinary within and beyond health sciences	Embraces a few disciplines but has not emphasized multidisciplinarity	Encourages multidisciplinarity approaches, particularly within health sciences and social sciences

One Health has a focus that is, at the same time, both broader and more specific: more specific in the sense that the OH approach focuses on the interconnectedness between human, animal (including wildlife and livestock), and environmental health, especially concerning zoonoses and ecosystem health; broader in the sense that it is aimed at improving not only human health, but also the health of non-human animals, as well as the maintenance of the environment and the ecosystem in general.

The two undoubtedly intersect and share common ground for action. For example, many global health challenges, such as pandemics (COVID-19, influenza), antimicrobial resistance, and emerging zoonoses, are directly related to the principles of One Health. Furthermore, implementing solutions within the framework of One Health (integrating veterinary health, human health, and environmental disciplines) strengthens global health efforts to prevent and control disease outbreaks.

With regard to their complementarities, global health provides a macro, systemic approach to health equity and policy, often addressing social and structural determinants, while One Health provides an operational, multidisciplinary approach to managing risks at the human–animal–environment interface. Together, they foster more effective, holistic strategies, for instance through joint surveillance, integrated responses, and multi-sectoral collaborations.

ONE HEALTH AND PLANETARY HEALTH

Compared to One Health, planetary health is a younger concept proposed in 2015 by the Rockefeller Foundation–Lancet Commission, coinciding with the launch of the UN Sustainable Development Goals. Here, planetary health is defined as:

> *the health of human civilisation and the state of the natural systems on which it depends. (Whithmee et al., 2015, p. 1978)*

In 2021, the planetary health alliance redefined planetary health as:

> *a solutions-oriented, transdisciplinary field and social movement focused on analyzing and addressing the impacts of human disruptions to Earth's natural systems on human health and all life on Earth.*[3]

After all, according to the World Health Organization, environmental degradation is responsible for nearly one fourth of all deaths and diseases worldwide (Hampshire et al., 2022).

One of the theories underlying the planetary health approach concerns the "planetary boundaries" proposed by the Stockholm Resilience Centre in 2009 (Rockstrom et al., 2009). To be precise, it is a framework rather than a theory, describing nine limits to the impacts of human activities on the Earth system. These are critical ecological boundaries beyond which the planet risks entering irreversible states of instability and transition that could jeopardize human living conditions and biodiversity. The authors argue that respecting these limits is essential to ensure sustainable development. Every system has an upper limit (boundary) which, if exceeded, can have catastrophic effects, such as positive feedback and global instability.

These nine boundaries are climate change, ocean acidification, stratospheric ozone depletion, biogeochemical flows in the nitrogen cycle, excess global freshwater use, land system change, the erosion of biosphere integrity, chemical pollution, and atmospheric aerosol loading. Some of these limits have already been exceeded (such as climate change and loss of biodiversity), increasing the risk of planetary crises.

With environmental issues like global warming and biodiversity decline accelerating, the field of planetary health highlights that safeguarding the environment is not just an ecological concern but a vital component of ensuring human health and societal stability. It calls for a paradigm shift from viewing human health and environmental health as separate issues to recognizing their profound interconnectedness and working toward sustainable, integrated solutions.

We can, therefore, see how planetary health has strong connections with One Health, under the assumption of the profound interconnection between environmental health and human health (to which One Health adds animal health). Moreover, both approaches emphasize the importance of sustainability (OH for future generations; planetary health for the "resilience" of the Earth System).

In Table 2, we have summarized the main features of One Health, global health, and planetary health.

Table 2. Main Features of One Health, Global Health, and Planetary Health.

Feature	One Health	Global Health	Planetary Health
Scope	Interconnections between human, animal (domestic and wild), and environmental health, focusing on disease prevention and ecosystem health	Overall health of populations worldwide, addressing health disparities, healthcare systems, and social determinants	The health of human civilization and the natural systems on which it depends, emphasizing sustainability of the planet's ecosystems and health
Primary focus	Zoonoses, environmental factors affecting health and ecosystem health through integrated approaches	Reducing global health disparities, disease control, strengthening health systems, and policy development	Sustainability of natural systems, climate change and biodiversity, and their impacts on human health and well-being
Disciplinary emphasis	Veterinary sciences, medicine, ecology, environmental sciences, public health, social sciences	Medicine, public health, epidemiology, social sciences, health policy	Environmental science, ecology, public health, sustainable development, social sciences
Ultimate goal	Prevent diseases transmitted between animals and humans; promote ecosystem health	Achieve health equity and improve health outcomes globally	Ensure sustainable development for human health without destroying natural systems; address climate change

(Continued)

Table 2. **(*Continued*)**

Feature	One Health	Global Health	Planetary Health
Approach	Integrative, transdisciplinary, and multisectoral, focusing on disease transmission, ecosystems, and biodiversity	Multisectoral, policy-driven, and focused on social determinants and healthcare systems	Holistic, emphasizing planetary boundaries, sustainability, and the interconnectedness of human and environmental health

To sum up:

- Global health concentrates on improving health equity and outcomes across populations worldwide, with a broad focus on health systems and social determinants.
- Planetary health expands the perspective to consider how the health of natural systems and planetary boundaries directly influence human health, emphasizing sustainability and environmental conservation.
- Until now, One Health has emphasized the health linkages between humans, animals, and ecosystems aimed at preventing zoonoses and environmental health threats.

An interesting proposal for integrating the three fields comes from Correira et al. (2021).

Correira et al. (2021) start out from a rhetorical question:

> *For us the question is not which of the three conceptual frameworks – Global Health or One Health or Planetary Health – best suits pandemic prevention and sustainable development. Rather, the question is if the concepts and related frameworks of Global, One and Planetary Health should stand as independent responses from each other to address the complex nature of the health problems and their determinants, as outlined by the 2030 agenda for sustainable development, or if we should aim at a progressive conceptual convergence and a wide and deep-rooted commitment to inter- and transdisciplinary actions around the Sustainable Development Goals. (Correira et al., 2021, p. 2)*

For Correira et al. (2021) global health should stand as an overarching concept embracing the attributes of One and planetary health. If my interpretation is correct, this is because the vision of global health contains a strong political dimension that can guide different policies and interventions related to human, animal, and environmental health. The different cognitive and intervention modalities linked to the three approaches should, therefore, be linked and connected in an integrated manner, with the awareness that

> *no human health and well-being is sustainable in time and space without a synergetic living with nature; that the intersection between human and nature can only be pursued if policy design and implementation builds on a global-scale understanding of trade, consumption, and economy. (Correira et al., 2021, p. 2)*

The vision of Correira et al. is undoubtedly promising. It also makes it clear how

> *we can climb out of the silos that we too often inhabit (Correira et al., 2024, p. 976).*

INTEGRATING ONE HEALTH WITH POST-COLONIAL HEALTH?

The post-colonial health approach is a critical approach. As should be clear by now, in social sciences, a critical approach means a perspective that opposes the neo-liberal economic system. For critical thinking, social institutions and their modes of organization are shaped to confirm and legitimize the status quo, that is, capitalism. Even health systems do not escape this logic, and indeed the Health Industrial Complex seeks to pursue profit, or in any case objectives that are far removed from authentic social justice.

This logic has also been "exported" to countries dependent on the United States, and on European countries before that. The "spirit of capitalism" has thus spread even to countries historically distant from this mercantile mode.

The "post-colonial" approach, in the field of global health, is, therefore, an anti-colonial approach. It analyzes and seeks to deconstruct the historical legacies and colonial power structures that continue to influence global health practices, policies, and priorities. It is necessary to recognize how colonialism, with its exploitation, oppression, and imposition of (market) value systems, has created and perpetuated health inequalities between and within nations. Here are some key elements of the post-colonial approach in global health:

Recognition of the historical context. The post-colonial approach begins with explicit recognition of how colonialism has shaped health systems, infrastructure, resource distribution and power dynamics globally. This also includes recognizing how colonial powers often exploited the natural and human resources of the countries they colonized, weakening their health systems and imposing development patterns that had negative consequences for health.

Decolonization of knowledge. The post-colonial approach questions the validity and neutrality of the knowledge produced by Western countries, often considered "universal" but actually based on specific cultural perspectives and values. Instead, it is necessary to value indigenous and local knowledge, recognizing that communities often have a deep understanding of their own health problems and the most appropriate solutions.

Central role of communities. The post-colonial approach affords a central role to communities impacted by health inequalities, acknowledging their right to self-determination and active participation in establishing priorities, designing interventions, and evaluating results. A paternalistic, "top-down" model is abandoned in favor of a participatory and community-led approach (see Chapter 6).

Equity and justice. The post-colonial approach aims to promote equity and justice in global health by addressing the root causes of health inequalities, such as poverty, inequality, discrimination, and lack of access to education and resources. It seeks to redistribute power and resources, ensuring that the most vulnerable communities have access to the care they need.

The One Health perspective is not exempt from criticism from the thinkers of post-colonial studies:

> *Like previous projects of the [Rockfeller] Foundation, Planetary Health and One Health can be read as proposals for preserving the capitalist order in the face of the perceived need for social change. More specifically, these two approaches pursue the prevention and control of environmental deterioration and animal diseases that impact human health, to avoid more instability in the capitalist order. (Baquero et al., 2021, p. 2)*

The way OH constructs its knowledge is also carefully scrutinized:

> *Much of One Health scholarship engages a naturalistic or realist ontology, where what appears to be simply is, without sufficient attention to epistemological questions of how knowledge of what "is" comes to be. Knowledge hierarchies privilege dominant science,*

> *and especially western "biomedical epistemology." Knowledges that fall outside of the realm of dominant science are not only devalued, but become unintelligible within a scientistic worldview. (Van Patter et al., 2023, p. 2)*

Precisely for this reason:

> *One Health is a conceptual framework that (...) brings together statements in favor of health for all, but in practice reinforces the myth of modernity. (Baquero et al., 2021, p. 7)*

At the heart of modernity is the individual, with his willpower and rationality. One of the frequently cited limitations of One Health is a pervasive anthropocentrism:

> *Linked to human exceptionalism and speciesism, anthropocentrism is a core feature of Eurocentric thought, and central to settler colonialism. (Van Patter et al., 2023, p. 1)*

Anthropocentrism also entails the impossibility of shifting one's point of view, and this is why post-colonial studies emphasize the central role of reflexivity. In other words, the post-colonial approach requires constant reflexivity on the part of health workers, researchers, and funders, who must examine their own prejudices, values, and their role in perpetuating health inequalities. It requires an awareness of power dynamics and a commitment to deconstructing colonial structures within not only one's own organizations, but also with regard to one's own living practices, and thus knowledge (Maccallum, 2025).

The post-colonial approach undoubtedly possesses a firm analytical methodology for critical analysis. As far as proposals are concerned, the idea of a One Health of Peripheries can be mentioned:

> *Extending the scope and the meaning of the Ottawa Charter proposal, the decolonial promotion of One Health of Peripheries comprise seven actions: (1) deconstruct apparatuses of marginalization; (2) enrich the ecology of knowledge; (3) build healthy multispecies public policy; (4) create supportive environments; (5) strengthen multispecies community actions; (6) develop individual capabilities in multiple species, and (7) reorient multispecies health services. (Baquero et al., 2021, p. 11)*

NOTES

1. For further details, see https://oneworldonehealth.wcs.org/about-us/mission/the-manhattan-principles.aspx.

2. See https://www.who.int/health-topics/one-health#tab=tab_1.

3. See https://planetaryhealthalliance.org/what-is-planetary-health/.

REFERENCES

Baquero, O. S., Fernàndez, M. N. B., & Aguilar, M. A. (2021). From modern Planetary Health to decolonial promotion of One Health of peripheries. *Frontiers in Public Health*, *10*(9), 637897. 10.3389/fpubh.2021.637897

Bryant, J. H., & Velji, A. (2011). Global Health: Evolving meanings. *Infectious Disease Clinics of North America*, *25*(2), 299–309. https://doi.org/10.1016/j.idc.2011.02.004

Correira, T., Ribeiro, C. T. D., & Ferrinho, P. (2021). Calling for a planetary and one health vision for global health. *One Health*, *13*, 1–3. https://doi.org/10.1016/j.onehlt.2021.100342

Correira, T., Ricciardi, W., & McKee, M. (2024). Preparing for the 'next pandemic': Why we need to escape from our silos. *The International Journal of Health Planning and Management*, *39*(4), 973–979. https://doi.org/10.1002/hpm.3757

FAO, OIE, WHO, Un System Influenza Coordination, UNICEF, THE WORLD BANK. (2008). *Contributing to One World, One Health* A strategic framework for reducing risks of infectious diseases at the animal–human–ecosystems interface*. https://www.fao.org/4/aj137e/aj137e00.pdf

Favretto, A., & Balduzzi, G. (2023). Giving meaning to action and research: Notes on the 'One Health' approach from a sociological perspective. *Development*, *66*, 226–232 https://doi.org/10.1057/s41301-023-00383-2

Ghebreyesus, T. D. (2021). *WHO Director-General's opening remarks at 27th tripartite annual executive committee meeting world organisation for animal health (OIE) – 17 February 2021*. https://www.who.int/director-general/speeches/detail/who-director-general-s-opening-remarks-at-27th-tripartite-annual-executive-committee-meeting-world-organisation-for-animal-health-oie-17-february-2021

Hampshire, K., Islam, N., Kissel, B., Chase, H., & Gundline, K. (2022). The Planetary Health report card: A student-led initiative to inspire planetary health in medical schools. *The Lancet*, *6*, e449–e454. https://doi.org/10.1016/S2542-5196(22)00045-6

Kickbush, I. (2006). The need for a European strategy on global health. *Scandinavian Journal of Public Health*, *34*(6), 561–565. https://doi.org/10.1080/14034940600973059

Kleinman, A. (2010). Four social theories for global health. *Lancet*, *1*(9725), 1518–1519. https://doi.org/10.1016/s0140-6736(10)60646-0

Koplan, P. J., Bond, T. C., Herson, M. H., Reddy, K. S., Rodriguez, M. H., Sewankambo, N., & Wesserheit. J., Consortium of Universities for Global Health Executive Board. (2009). Towards a common definition of global health. *Lancet*, *6*(9679), 1993–1995. https://doi.org/10.1016/S0140-6736(09)60332-9

Maccallum, E. (2025). *La salute dei corpi periferici oltre One Health: verso una giustizia olistica e anticoloniale* [The health of peripherical bodies beyond One Health: Towards an anti-colonial and holistic justice]. Bachelor dissertation, Sociology Program, Università di Bologna.

Merson, M. H., Black, R. E., & Mills, A. J. (2006). Introduction. In M. H. Merson, R. E. Black, & A. J. Mills (Eds.), *International public health: Diseases, programs, systems, and policies*. Jones and Bartlett Publishers.

One Health High-Level Expert Panel (OHHLEP). (2022). One Health: A new definition for a sustainable and healthy future. *PLoS Pathogens*, *18*(6), e1010537. 10.1371/journal.ppat.1010537

Pettan-Brewer, C., Penn, G., Biondo, A. W., Jaenisch, T., Grützmache, K., & Kahn, L. H. (2024). Who coined the term "One Health"? Cooperation amid the siloization. *One Health*, *12*(18). https://doi.org/10.1016/j.onehlt.2024.100678

Rockstrom, J., Steffen, W., Noone, K., Perrson, A., Chapin, F. S., & Foley, J. (2009). Planetary boundaries: Exploring the safe operating space for humanity. *Ecology and Society*, *14*(2), 32. http://www.ecologyandsociety.org/vol14/iss2/art32/

Sundberg J. P., & Schofield P. N. (2009). One medicine, one pathology, and the one health concept. *Journal of American Veterinarian Medical Association*, *15*(12), 1530–1531. doi: 10.2460/javma.234.12.1530.

Van Patter, E. V., Linares-Roake, J., & Breen, V. A. (2023). What does One Health want? Feminist, posthuman, and anti-colonial possibilities. *One Health Outlook*, *5*(1), 4. https://doi.org/10.1186/s42522-022-00076-9

Whithmee, S., Haines, A., Beyrer, C., Boltz, F., Capon, A., Yach, D. (2015). Safeguarding human health in the Anthropocene epoch: Report of The Rockefeller Foundation–Lancet Commission on planetary health. *The Lancet*, *386*, 1973–2028. https://doi.org/10.1016/S0140-6736(15)60901-1

Winslow, C. E. (1920). The untilled fields of Public Health. *Science*, *9*(1306), 23–33. https://doi.org/10.1126/science.51.1306.23

2

LIVING IN THE RISK SOCIETY

ABSTRACT

This chapter explores the pivotal role of risk in contemporary social sciences, drawing on the seminal theoretical contributions of Ulrich Beck and Anthony Giddens. Within an increasingly interconnected and complex global context, uncertainty is governed and partly rendered measurable through the notion of risk. Nevertheless, the chapter argues that risk management alone cannot suffice and should be accompanied by trust, understood as a positive future-oriented expectation that makes action possible in a high-risk society. These analytical perspectives are then applied to the One Health (OH) framework, highlighting how global challenges – such as the excessive use of antibiotics in animal production contributing to antimicrobial resistance – generate intricate, interlinked, and often imperceptible risks affecting human, animal, and environmental health. The discussion further considers the growing erosion of public trust in science, exemplified by vaccine hesitancy and distorted interpretations of health risks, which obstruct the effective implementation of OH strategies. The chapter ultimately calls for the integration of social sciences within OH surveillance in order to foster community support, trust, and engagement and offer sociological knowledge for targeted interventions, thereby strengthening institutional actions that acknowledge and address the interconnected nature of health.

Keywords: Risk society; trust; antimicrobial resistance; vaccine hesitancy; health risks; community support

INTRODUCTION

We live in an increasingly interdependent world. It used to be said that a flutter of wings in Australia can cause a blizzard in Sweden. While this theory is difficult to verify, we do know for sure that a financial crisis in the United States today may cause mortgage interest rates to rise in Italy and thus make life difficult for young couples in Florence, perhaps dissuading them from having children that year and – who knows? – maybe even the following years. There is, therefore, a three-step causal sequence between a few weeks of financial turmoil on Wall Street and the birth rate in Italy.

In the highly complex, uncertain situation we live in, the future can take many forms, partly as a consequence of our choices, and partly for reasons beyond our control. We live in a world dominated by risk.

The concept of risk has a central place in social sciences. That is why this work will be looking over a number of sociological approaches that have placed risk at the center of their explanatory models. We will be specifically focusing on Ulrick Beck and Anthony Giddens. Roughly speaking, we could say that the uncertainty that dominates contemporary life can be reduced through the concept of risk. Turning uncertainty into (quantifiable) risk is not sufficient, however. We will then move on to analyze "the other side of the coin," that is, the concept of trust, without which we cannot act in the risk society. Trust is a positive expectation about the future that enables us to do things. This is why we will be looking at some types of trust proposed by the Polish sociologist Sztompka. We will then be turning our focus to trust in science, or perhaps it would be better to say distrust in science. Nowadays, for various reasons, science is not in great shape, complex though the question is. For one thing, vaccines brought us out of COVID-19, yet trust in vaccines has declined consistently since the COVID-19 period. We will then move on to discuss the main reflections and explanations relating to distrust in science, with a particular focus on medicine, and the "death of expertise." We will be illustrating how the sociological concepts proposed in this chapter can be connected to the One Health paradigm and in which aspects of One Health they can be employed.

THE DOMINANCE OF RISK IN CONTEMPORARY SOCIETY

Ulrich Beck constructed the most important sociological theory of risk. The theory is set out in *Risk Society* (Beck, 1992). In his view, risk is not merely a statistical probability of negative outcomes, but a social and cultural construct that reflects the complexity and uncertainties of modern life. Beck argues that risk is shaped by social processes, cultural norms, and public perceptions. It is also influenced by societal values, scientific knowledge, and political contexts. As far back as the 1990s, Beck noted the "glocal" dimension of risk (although he does not use this term). Indeed, as Steven Mithen writes, inspired by Beck:

> *What is remarkable about our current situation is the extent to which the global and the local intertwine. Decisions made at global altitude – for, example, about international trading, nuclear power or global warming – produce knock on consequences for local activities. Similarly, local practices – overproduction, regional conflict or the production of poisonous emissions – generate consequences which impact in distant regions. (Mithen, 2004, p. 5)*

Paradoxically, knowledge is the source of risks, not ignorance. The modernization process creates new hazards and uncertainties, largely because of the unintended consequences of the use of scientific knowledge to control nature: "Science is no longer concerned with liberation from pre-existing dependencies, but with the definition and distribution of errors which are produced by itself" (Beck, 1992, p. 158). The risk society theory starts from a historical reconstruction that considers three different types of social exposure to risk.

The first is the pre-modern phase, in which there are hazards believed to derive from external forces such as nature or supernatural entities (gods or demons): phenomena such as famines, droughts, or epidemics. Then comes the modern or industrial phase (beginning around 1850 and ending just over a hundred years later). In this phase, external risks coexist with humanly produced dangers such as smoking, drinking, and occupational injuries. The risk society emerges with the increasing importance of science and technology in economic activities and everyday life. Risk is, therefore, produced by the increase in knowledge. In other words, this is a society of manufactured risks: air pollution, chemical warfare, nuclear power plants. Risks are self-generated by man. Moreover potential hazards of late modern technologies are:

> *(1) global in their potential consequences (e.g., nuclear disasters or pollution), (2) difficult to perceive without relying on the expertise of the very institutions that created the hazard (e.g., chemists must test for chemical pollutants), and (3) arise not from a lack of resources as with previous hazards (e.g., famine) but rather from an abundance of unwanted consequences arising from modern technologies (e.g., cancer due to exposure to air pollution). (Mythen, 2004, p. 141)*

More specifically, for Beck (2008), risk in contemporary society is characterized by "delocalization." The delocalization of risks occurs on three levels:

- *Spatial*: the new risks (e.g., climate change) are spreading over national borders, and even over continents;
- *Temporal*: the new risks (e.g., nuclear waste) have a long latency period, so their future effects cannot be reliably determined and restricted; moreover, knowledge and non-knowing are changing, so the question of who is affected is itself temporally open and remains disputed;
- *Social*: since the new risks (e.g., financial crises) are the result of complex processes involving long chains of effects, their causes and effects cannot be determined with sufficient precision.

One concept Beck insists on is that of reflexivity, that is, the continuous monitoring of one's actions in order to intervene if things do not go as planned. Reflexivity characterizes both the actions of large organizations and the actions of individuals. The complexity of social life compels us to observe our own behavior and that of others in order to navigate contingencies and modify both our actions and, in many instances, our goals. Then, at the level of risk perception, advancements in knowledge have failed to result in a more secure social climate (van Loon, 2002, p. 173). Indeed, "individuals in the West live comparatively longer and healthier lives, while simultaneously feeling less safe and secure" (Mythen, 2004, p. 3).

The sociologist Anthony Giddens writes in the same years as Ulrich Beck. Some of their positions are similar. Giddens undoubtedly places greater emphasis on the role of trust and expert systems.

The concept of risk is central in Giddens' theory. Giddens notes that even though the concept of risk has been a part of the modernization process, it has now acquired a peculiar position. The word risk was originally connected to the explorers who sailed in unknown and dangerous seas: in other words, it referred to places. After a while, however, the word started to be connected to time instead of place. Risk became a category of banking and insurance and was used to indicate the probability of some events happening. Risk was the means by which the future could be faced.

Today, however, our attempts to control the future are ineffective and we need new ways to treat new uncertainties. Giddens (1999) suggests considering two kinds of risks: external risk and manufactured risk. External risks are risks coming from "outside," mainly from nature, while manufactured risks are the products of the impact of human knowledge and capacities on the world. According to Giddens, when we started to be worried about what we could do against nature, instead of what nature can do against us, we moved from the dominance of external risks to the dominance of manufactured risks. External risks, which dominated the industrial society, are concerned with the possibility of individuals to be involved in unexpected events, even if such events could be anticipated in some ways. Insurance is the answer to external risks: the welfare state, an insurance against illness and unemployment, is the example given by Giddens. Manufactured risks, which are a product of late modernity, are concerned with catastrophes in the natural and social environment. They arise from technological and scientific development and have unanticipated consequences.

The multiplication of risks has resulted in the growth of expert systems. Giddens notes that as societies become more complex, they increasingly depend on specialized, technical, and scientific expertise – that is, *expert systems* – to make informed decisions about risks and social issues. However, Giddens points out that expert systems also concentrate knowledge power. As decision-making increasingly depends on experts, questions of who controls and has access to specialized knowledge become central to social and political relations.

THE OTHER SIDE OF THE COIN: TRUST

In sociology, the concept of trust originates from Durkheim's and Simmel's theories, yet, in the contemporary debate, it did not acquire a remarkable epistemic status until after Luhmann (1968). Consistently with his view, Luhmann proposes a functionalistic concept of trust. For Luhmann, trust has the function of reducing complexity. Trust can be considered an antidote of uncertainty, which allows us to undertake risky actions. Trust is, therefore, an operational relief: being doubtful of everything brings paralyzing effects. Trust enables us to treat the (unknown) future as if it were the (known) present: we trust that the WiFi will work when we switch on our laptop in the morning; we trust shops to be open during business hours; we trust that our plane won't fall out of the sky and that water will come out of the bathroom tap. So together with Luhmann, we may define trust as a positive expectation formulated in uncertain conditions on cognitive and emotional grounds. Hope is different from trust. Hope seems to be a sort of paler, more blurred expectation compared to trust. According to Sztompka (1995), hope is connected with those events that men cannot modify and which, once they have happened, they can only adjust to, while trust describes our attitude toward those events produced by human actions. Trust, insofar as we can control other people's actions, seems to be more "reassuring" compared to mere hope. In brief, we can say that trust refers to human actions, while hope refers to natural events. Trust and hope, respectively, are the answers to the risk/danger distinction. Together with Douglas (1992), we can assume that risks are the outcome of human actions, while danger has to do with the unpredictability of nature.

In other words, the distinction between risk and danger is based on the damage a person (or another entity) can suffer in the future. If damage can be seen as a consequence of a decision of ours, then we can speak about risk; if damage is caused by something beyond our will, something "external," then we can speak about danger.

Once, falling ill with cancer was a danger; nowadays, thanks to screening technology, falling ill with cancer has, in many cases, become a risk of failure in prevention.[1]

Moreover, the inclination to take risks is much stronger than the inclination to face dangers depending on other people's decisions: reckless drivers may feel very uncomfortable when someone else (even a more careful driver) is behind the wheel. Chain-smokers may be much more worried about the air they breathe in town than the damage smoking can cause.

The risk/danger distinction is similar to the one proposed by Beck and Giddens between external risk and manufactured risk.

The four concepts we have proposed can also be related as follows:

Trust: Risk = Hope: Danger

Trust concerns risks and, therefore, a kind of "calculability"; hope concerns danger and therefore the obligation to rely on fate or destiny. Sztompka, from a different perspective (1995), identifies seven kinds of trust:

1. *Generalized trust*, that is, trust in social order itself or trust in a particular form of social order: "Canada is a great society!."

2. *Segmental trust*, that is, trust in institutional segments of society such as the economy, education, justice: "The Swedish health care system is highly developed!."

3. *Technological trust*, that is, trust in technical systems such as financial markets, transport systems, telecommunications.

4. *Organizational trust*, that is, trust in organizations such as universities, corporations, or a particular hospital. When trust is given to political organizations such as the government or parliament, we can speak about public trust.

5. *Commercial trust*, that is, trust in goods that are an answer to human needs. This kind of trust can have a high degree of generalization – "Japanese cars are very safe!" – or a low one: "A book written by Umberto Eco must be very exciting!."

6. *Positional trust*, that is, trust given to particular social roles: judges, doctors, priests, etc.

7. *Personal trust*, that is, trust given to someone we consider "special": a friend, a teacher, etc. Trust given to relatives can be called private trust.

These forms of trust are of course to be regarded as ideal categories. It is not difficult to see how in reality, overlaps and ambiguities are very frequent. However, distinguishing between objects of trust allows for a more precise analysis.

According to Sztompka, trust spreads from the top down, while mistrust spreads from the bottom up. To summarize, a high generalized trust, which is a high level of trust in the institutions, will in turn produce trust in particular social roles, and this trust will eventually filter down to the lowest levels, that is, to people in social relationships. In contrast, if we do not trust people and social roles, this kind of mistrust will eventually impact society as a whole. In addition, there is a third icastic statement to bear in mind:

> *trust is easier to transform into distrust than is distrust into trust. (Luhmann, 1979, p. 89)*

This lapidary, seraphic phrase can be understood by including the temporal dimension in our reflections. Trust is not created, it is built slowly. The transition from distrust to trust takes time, and one attempt is not enough. In Italian, we say: "One swallow doesn't make a summer." Conversely, a rich, lengthy love story can collapse in a day due to the betrayal of a partner.

TRUST IN SCIENCE AND TECHNOLOGY

According to the Pew Center, in 2023:

> *overall 57% of Americans say science has had a mostly positive effect on society. This share is down 8 percentage points since November 2021 and down 16 points since before the start of the coronavirus outbreak. (Pew, 2023, p. 4)*

Moreover,

> *when it comes to the standing of scientists, 73% of U.S. adults have a great deal or fair amount of confidence in scientists to act in the public's best interests. But trust in scientists is 14 points lower than it was at the early stages of the pandemic. The share expressing the strongest level of trust in scientists – saying they have a great deal of confidence in them – has fallen from 39% in 2020 to 23% today [2023]. (Pew, 2023, p. 4)*

In 2018, the American Society of Clinical Oncology's second annual National Cancer Opinion Survey showed that nearly 4 in 10 US citizens (39%) believed cancer can be tackled with alternative therapies such as enzyme and oxygen therapy, diet, vitamins, and minerals alone (ASCO's, 2019).

This loss of trust in science does not only regard the United States. In 2010, Heidi Larson established the Vaccine Confidence Project (VPC) at the London School of Hygiene and Tropical Medicine. The aim of this project is to gain a better understanding of growing vaccine skepticism around the world. The VPC was the first research group to map and monitor public confidence in vaccination at a global scale and remains the only research group fully dedicated to understanding the roots, trends over time, and impact of vaccine confidence (Larson et al., 2010).

In 2015, they introduced the Vaccine Confidence Index, a tool for gaining data-led insights into vaccine confidence at global, regional, and national levels. Comparing data on trust in vaccines in the years 2018 and 2023 shows a clear trend: trust in vaccines is in sharp decline worldwide, with a few exceptions. If we compare the answers to the statement: "Vaccines are important for children," we can observe a decline in trust in 49 states out of 65 from 2018 (Larson et al., 2010).

The growing distrust in science stems from a number of causes, which are not always easily separable. These causes do not all have the same solidity.

The first cause of the current mistrust in science is the ease with which the internet allows access to scientific information, knowledge, and notions. The problem is that much of this information is wrong. There used to be more trust in science because of the material difficulty in accessing knowledge, which required buying books and spending many hours reading them. This is why it was easier to rely on scientists. In the 1970s in the United States, there was more trust in science by people with conservative political views than by liberals, who had more critical attitudes. On internet, it is difficult to establish a hierarchy with regard to the validity of knowledge, and our bubble will tend to confirm our beliefs:

> *we all live in an epistemic bubble that largely determines what information (and, even more critically, misinformation) reaches us. (Contessa, 2022, p. 13)*

This brings us to the second point: it is very easy for internet to create pseudo-scientific communities of thought: collective intelligences that reinforce their beliefs with seemingly rational arguments supported by data selected *ad hoc*. Through careful cherry-picking, data can be made to say anything, even that smoking does not cause lung cancer. According to Gawande:

> *Science's defenders have identified five hallmark moves of pseudoscientists. They argue that the scientific consensus emerges from a conspiracy to suppress dissenting views. They produce fake experts, who have views contrary to established knowledge but do not actually have a credible scientific track record. They cherry-pick the data and papers that challenge the dominant view as a means of discrediting an entire field. They deploy false analogies and other logical fallacies. And they set impossible expectations of research: when scientists produce one level of certainty, the pseudoscientists insist they achieve another. (Gawande, 2016)*

Third, paradoxical though it may sound, much of the distrust in science does not stem from distrust in science *tout court*. It stems from distrust in *this* science. This is the problem with the idealization of science. Many people portray science "as free of interests, exclusively devoted to the good of humanity and designed to achieve objective knowledge" and any deviation from this idyllic vision is considered a betrayal (Neresini, 2024, p. 45).

The idea is mainly that economic forces secretly conspire to influence scientific procedures – such as clinical trials – to serve their own interests. According to Contessa:

> *private funding influences biomedical research negatively in two ways – it biases it (as it creates a conflict of interest for the researchers, who are funded by the very corporations that stand to gain or lose financially from their research), and it skews it (as it promotes certain research directions (such as, e.g., development of new patentable drugs) over others (such as, e.g., research on off-label uses of old drugs, non-pharmaceutical interventions, or lifestyle changes) on the basis of considerations of profitability. (Contessa, 2022, pp. 11–12)*

However, bribes to falsify results regarding a drug's efficacy are one thing and huge investments to produce common cold medicines at the expense of serious but unprofitable rare diseases are quite another. The former is a serious crime, the latter a legitimate (albeit cynical) industrial choice. The problem is that science is not based on an unambiguous procedure that follows rigorous steps to reach objective and definitive truths. Even in the choice of its object of study, scientific discovery is influenced by economic, social, and historical factors and proceeds through compromises and negotiations. And it reaches partial truths, related to the context and even to how it is communicated. In summary,

> *knowledge is not a static description of reality but the emerging result of ongoing processes to which many heterogeneous actors contribute and on which they also depend. (Neresini, 2024, p. 34)*

To return to the causes of declining public trust in science, there are three other factors to be mentioned. While perhaps less significant than the preceding three, these factors are undoubtedly incisive: the complexity of scientific communication, the presence of conflicting scientific positions, and rapid technological change. Let us look at them in more detail.

Popularizing science is difficult because science is complex. Sometimes it is not possible to avoid the use of technical language, and references to data may require some statistical expertise. In addition, communication has to be gauged toward an "average" recipient that does not exist, with the strong possibility of making it trivial for the lay expert and difficult for people with little education or educational backgrounds far removed from that field of study. Last but not least, scientific findings often involve uncertainties, which can be misinterpreted as incoherence or weakness (the opposite of the idea people generally have of science). For example, this is often the case in nutritional science, where studies sometimes give conflicting dietary recommendations, creating confusion among the public. To cite other specific cases, some studies claim moderate alcohol consumption reduces heart disease risk, while others find no benefit or even increased risk, leading to mixed messages about alcohol intake. Or we could mention the area of mental illness, where for some, ADHD does not exist, while for others, it is a serious threat to young people today. Moreover, those who recognize its existence are divided on how it should be dealt with (mainly by pharmacological means or using psychotherapy).

Another aspect that undermines people's trust in science, and which overlaps with the former two, concerns rapid technological change. For example, the advent of genetically modified organisms has led to public debate and mistrust fueled by rapid scientific advancements outpacing regulatory and public understanding.

The philosopher Elisabetta Lalumera, taking up some reflections by Onora O'Neill, identifies four components underlying relationships of trust. The first is the existence of a need on the part of those who have to trust (e.g., the need to be treated because they are ill). The second is the "epistemic" component: we trust if we attribute competence and expertise to the object of trust (be it an institution or a person). The third is the "values" component: I trust a person or an institution that is oriented toward good. The fourth is the component that regards limitations to trust: I trust the doctor for matters concerning health, but not, for example, for my home renovation plans. Lalumera applies this model to the crisis in the relationship between the individual citizen and the healthcare system. She notes that in the case of the epistemic component:

> *we find it increasingly difficult in public debate to admit that someone, by virtue of their institutional role, knows more than we do. Without going as far as grandiloquently citing the "death of expertise," in the internet age, the citizen wants to check the epistemic credentials of the experts, including doctors and healthcare professionals. (Lalumera, 2021, p. 82)*

Second, with regard to the values component and thus the good pursued, there is little to be optimistic about:

> *given the cases of corruption in scientific institutions and even more so in the management of healthcare institutions. Another significant phenomenon is the marketization of hospitals, the rationalization of resources in the national healthcare system that often results in fewer services being provided: hence the suspicion that the aim of the system is to save money and not – again – to do good. (Lalumera, 2021, p. 83)*

To these components, Lalumera adds the politicization of science and health and here; as an example, we could mention the aversion of American conservative groups to climate change and vaccines.

VACCINE HESITANCY AND ONE HEALTH

The growing distrust in science can be exemplified, as we have already mentioned, by the increase in vaccine hesitancy. Despite the relevance of vaccines in preserving health, there is a concerning growth of vaccine hesitancy among the population. According to the WHO, vaccine hesitancy can be considered: "delay in acceptance or refusal of vaccines despite availability of vaccination services" (WHO, 2014). The SAGE Working Group defines vaccine hesitancy as "the reluctance or refusal to vaccinate despite the availability of vaccines," noting it as a significant barrier to achieving vaccination coverage (MacDonald, 2015, p. 4116).

The COVID-19 pandemic has brought vaccine hesitancy back into focus. However, this is not a new issue. In many developed countries, a significant number of people are hesitant to get vaccinated against diseases, such as measles and rubella, that vaccines can prevent, especially in children. In 2019, the WHO named vaccine hesitancy as one of the top 10 threats to global health (WHO, 2019).

The public perception of the importance of vaccines for children declined during the COVID-19 pandemic in 52 out of 55 countries studied, UNICEF warned in a report on immunization released in 2023 (UNICEF, 2023). In the United States, about 1 in 5 children had parents reporting VH from 2019 to 2022 (Vashist et al., 2024). In Japan, "The vaccine crisis from 2013 to 2019 is predicted to result in an additional 24,600–27,300 cases and 5000–5700 deaths over the lifetime of cohorts born between 1994 and 2007, compared with if coverage had remained at around 70% since 2013" (Simms et al., 2020, p. e223).

There is a direct link between One Health and vaccine hesitancy. One Health emphasizes the connection between human, animal, and environmental health. Vaccine hesitancy in veterinary medicine can disrupt these connections by increasing the risk of disease transmission across species. As vaccines are crucial for controlling zoonotic diseases, hesitancy undermines these efforts, increasing the potential for outbreaks. Due to the increasing human vaccine hesitancy, a spillover into veterinary medicine can occur: those who are more likely to hesitate to get vaccinations for themselves or family members are more likely to hesitate also for their dogs or cats (Lederhouse, 2024). According to Heidi Larson and other colleagues, this is due to factors such as "a decline in the public's trust of experts, preferences for alternative health, political polarization, and belief-based extremism" (Larson et al., 2022, p. 58).

Studies have identified multiple factors influencing VH, including socioeconomic status, education level, trust in the healthcare system.

There are also interesting psychological theories regarding vaccine hesitancy:

> *When facing complex decision-making processes, individuals use intuitive, automatic, and often unconscious strategies to address*

> *an issue more easily. For example, when deciding to follow the vaccination program, research has shown that individuals are more averse to take a risk associated with an action – inoculation of a possibly "unsafe" vaccine – than to take the risk associated with inaction, taking the chances of contracting a vaccine-preventable disease. This is known as omission bias. Additionally, individuals show a misunderstanding of co-occurrence with causation, also labelled as co-incidence bias, attributing every event occurring after immunization to be caused by vaccination. (Carlson et al., 2025, p. 2)*

MacDonald (2015), to analyze the phenomenon of vaccine hesitancy, propose the "3 Cs" model: Confidence, Complacency, Convenience.

Confidence is defined as trust in (i) the effectiveness and safety of vaccines; (ii) the system that delivers them, including the reliability and competence of the health services and health professionals; and (iii) the motivations of policymakers who decide on the vaccines needed.

Vaccination *complacency* exists where perceived risks of vaccine-preventable diseases are low, and vaccination is not deemed a necessary preventive action. Complacency about a particular vaccine or about vaccination in general is influenced by many factors, including other life/health responsibilities that may be seen to be more important at that point in time.

Vaccination *convenience* is a significant factor when physical availability, affordability, and willingness to pay, geographical accessibility, ability to understand (language and health literacy) and appeal of immunization services affect uptake. The quality of the service (real and/or perceived) and the degree to which vaccination services are delivered at a time and place and in a cultural context that is convenient and comfortable also affect the decision to be vaccinated and could lead to vaccine hesitancy.

In the post-COVID-19 scenario, Galagali et al. (2022) bring two additional C's to the attention of readers: Communication and Context.

Vaccination communication: Repeated risk communication is crucial to facilitate informed decision-making regarding VH. It is important to let the families and friends know the importance of the greater societal benefits of population-level immunity and the protection it offers to those who are vulnerable.

Vaccination context: The communication needs to take into account the recognition of context, including ethnicity, religion, occupation, and socio-economic status.

Countering vaccine hesitancy is certainly a daunting task, especially where – even in institutional contexts – doubts are raised about the efficacy and even the harmfulness of immunization. The politicization of health diminishes trust in medicine. Addressing vaccine hesitancy is vital within the One Health paradigm because it directly affects the success of integrated strategies to prevent and control zoonotic and infectious diseases across humans, animals, and ecosystems. Building trust and culturally sensitive communication are key to advancing both goals. However, this can only be done in a system of health governance that supports public health and recognizes the interdependent nature of health.

WHY THE RISK SOCIETY IS CONNECTED TO ONE HEALTH

The risk society is closely linked to the One Health perspective. As mentioned, the risks today are global. We live in an increasingly globalized, connected, and interdependent world. Globalization has radically catalyzed the everyday movement of people, animals, technology, goods, capital, and services worldwide. Thus, the risks of disease transmission increase not only geographically, but also between species.

Causal chains and interdependence are undoubtedly linked to the COVID-19 pandemic. Zoonosis, from which COVID-19 originated, is the clearest example of the connection between animal health and human health. Other diseases such as avian influenza (H5N1, H7N9), rabies, salmonellosis, Ebola, Lyme disease, bovine tuberculosis, brucellosis, toxoplasmosis, and yellow fever are also mostly transmitted via zoonoses. We can list four factors that increase the possibility of zoonosis. These causes can be reduced to economic and political choices linked to neo-liberalism, so they have nothing to do with biology and everything to do with society.

The primary causes of the increase in zoonoses are deforestation and urbanization. They are due to human intervention in the environment. So the environment–animals–man connection is glaringly evident. Urbanization brings with it a rise in population density, another factor that increases the risk of epidemics. Notice how there is a clear human influence on the environment and that the anthropization of the natural environment is driven by political choices or economic reasons. The same can be said of intensive livestock farming, another cause of the increasing transmission of pathogens between animals and humans. After all:

> *Per capita meat consumption has rapidly expanded over the last half century, driving the development of high-density livestock operations that provide opportunities for large-scale animal disease outbreaks. (Saylors et al., 2021, p. 2)*

Climate change, by causing alterations in animal habitats that in turn influence the distribution of vectors such as mosquitoes and ticks, is also linked to zoonoses. Again, even a superficial explanation is sufficient to identify social and economic causes (in short: neo-liberalism) behind global warming and thus the zoonoses, one of the many phenomena caused by climate change. The fourth factor is antimicrobial resistance. The overuse of antibiotics in animal husbandry encourages the development of resistant bacteria that, through the zoonotic chain, can also impact humans, complicating the prevention and treatment of infections.

In this context, the increasing decline in trust in science and medicine that can be observed globally, together with distorted perceptions of health risks, also complicates the implementation of policies and interventions based on the One Health approach, which – because it often focuses on preventive interventions that are seemingly far removed from obvious health problems – may not be immediately understood by the population. Integrating the social sciences One Health surveillance approach can provide several benefits:

> *building support, trust, and buy-in of populations hosting or involved in One Health initiatives; contributing sociological and anthropological insights on human activities to guide geographic targeting of surveillance initiatives; crafting "empathetic approaches" to behavioral interventions – either to mitigate outbreak risk or respond to outbreaks; and designing and implementing One Health interventions among at-risk populations. (Saylors et al., 2021, p. 16)*

However, as we have already pointed out, it is crucial for the institutional framework to support and promote interventions that recognize the centrality of public health and the interconnected nature of health, illustrating and intervening in the different dimensions of human, environmental, and animal health.

NOTE

1. I am of course aware of how social inequalities affect the possibility of carrying out prevention activities, and poverty could make cancer a danger rather than a risk once again.

REFERENCES

ASCO's. (2019). *ASCO's second national cancer opinion survey results: Surprising number of Americans believe alternative therapies can cure cancer*. https://connection.asco.org/do/second-asco-national-cancer-opinion-survey-results

Beck, U. (1992). *Risk society: Towards a new modernity*. Sage Publications.

Beck, U. (2008). World at risk: The new task of critical theory. *Development and Society*, *37*(1), 1–21.

Carlson, J. I., Puppo, F., Roca-Umbert, A., Folkvord, F., & Lupiáñez-Villanueva, F. (2025). *An experimental study on the effects of electronic medicinal product information on vaccine hesitancy*. Scientific Reports. https://doi.org/10.1038/s41598-025-96092-6

Contessa, G. (2022). It takes a village to trust science: Towards a (thoroughly) social approach to public trust in science. *Erkenntnis*, *17*, 1–26. https://doi.org/10.1007/s10670-021-00485-8

Douglas, M. (1992). *Risk and blame*. Routledge.

Galagali, P. M., Kinikar, A. A., & Kumar, V. S. (2022). Vaccine hesitancy: Obstacles and challenges. *Current Pediatrics Reports*, *10*(4), 241–248. https://doi.org/10.1007/s40124-022-00278-9

Gawande, A. (2016). *The mistrust of science*. New Desk – The New Yorker 100. Retrieved June 10, 2016, from https://www.newyorker.com/news/news-desk/the-mistrust-of-science

Giddens, A. (1999). Risk and responsibility. *The Modern Law Review*, *62*(1), 1–10. https://doi.org/10.1111/1468-2230.00188

Lalumera, E. (2021). Ricostruire la fiducia nel dibattito pubblico in materia di sanità. *Il Mulino Magazine*, *70*(4), 78–87.

Larson, H. J., Brocard, P., & Garnett, G. (2010). The India HPV-vaccine suspension. *Lancet*, *376*(9741), 572–573. https://doi.org/10.1016/S0140-6736(10)60881-1

Larson, H. J., Gakidou, E., & Murray, C. J. L. (2022). The vaccine-hesitant moment. *The New England Journal of Medicine*, *387*(1), 58–65. https://doi.org/10.1056/NEJMra2106441

Lederhouse, C. (2024). *Vaccine hesitancy gives some US dog, cat owners cold feet. Veterinarians find themselves combating misinformation and *educating clients on benefits of preventive medicine*. American Veterinary Medical Association (AVMA). Retrieved May 15, 2025, from https://www.avma.org/news/vaccine-hesitancy-gives-some-us-dog-cat-owners-cold-feet

Luhmann, N. (1968). *Vertrauen: ein Mechanismus der Reduktion sozialer Komplexität*. Ferdinand Enke Verlag; trad. It. (2002). La fiducia. Bologna: Il Mulino.

Luhmann, N. (1979). *Trust and power: Two works*. Wiley.

MacDonald, N. E. (2015). Vaccine hesitancy: Definition, scope and determinants. *Vaccine*, *33*(34), 4161–4164. https://doi.org/10.1016/j.vaccine.2015.04.036

Mythen, S. (2004). *After the ice: A global human history, 20,000–5000 BC*. Weidenfeld & Nicolson.

Neresini, F. (2024). Can we look at refused knowledge differently? In *Manufacturing refused knowledge in the age of epistemic pluralism. Discourses, imaginaries, and practices*.

Neresini, F., Agodi, M. C., Crabu, S., & Tosoni, S. (Eds.), *On the border of science*. Palgrave Macmillan. https://doi.org/10.1007/978-981-99-7188-6

Pew Research Center. (2023). *Americans' trust in scientists, positive views of science continue to decline*. Pew Research Center. Retrieved November 14, 2023, from https://www.pewresearch.org/science/2023/11/14/americans-trust-in-scientists-positive-views-of-science-continue-to-decline/

Saylors, K., Wolking, D. J., Hagan, E., Martinez, S., Francisco, L., ... Mazet, J. A. K. (2021). Socializing One Health: An innovative strategy to investigate social and behavioral risks of emerging viral threats. *One Health Outlook*, *3*(11). https://doi.org/10.1186/s42522-021-00036-9

Simms, K. T., Hanley, S. J. B., Smith, M. A., Keane, A., & Canfell, K. (2020). Impact of HPV vaccine hesitancy on cervical cancer in Japan: A modelling study. *Lancet Public Health*, *5*(4), e223–e234. https://doi.org/10.1016/S2468-2667(20)30010-4

Sztompka, P. (1995). *The sociology of social change*. Blackwell.

UNICEF (2023). *The state of the world's children 2023. For every child, vaccination*. https://www.unicef.org/reports/state-worlds-children-2023

Van Loon, S. (2002). *Risk and technological change*. Routledge.

Vashist, K., Yankey, D., Elam-Evas, L. D., Mu, Y., Valier, M. R., ... Singleton, J. A. (2024). Changes in vaccine hesitancy among parents of children aged 6 months – 17 Years, National Immunization Surveys, 2019–2022. *Vaccine*, *42*(20). https://doi.org/10.1016/j.vaccine.2024.05.037

WHO. (2014). *SAGE working group dealing with vaccine hesitancy (March 2012 to November 2014)*. World Health Organization. https://www.who.int/groups/strategic-advisory-group-of-experts-on-immunization/working-groups/vaccine-hesitancy-march-2012-to-november-2014

WHO. (2019). *Ten threats to global health in 2019*. World Health Organization. https://www.who.int/news-room/spotlight/ten-threats-to-global-health-in-2019

3

PROSPECTS FOR THE FUTURE: THEORIES AND METHODOLOGIES TO PREVENT ANOTHER PANDEMIC

ABSTRACT

This chapter explores how the One Health (OH) approach can be strengthened through sociological theories of non-knowledge and futures-oriented methodologies. While OH is valued for its capacity to anticipate ecological and health crises by viewing human, animal, and environmental systems as interdependent, it lacks a clear methodological framework for forecasting. The chapter first examines "undone science" and the sociology of ignorance, showing how gaps in knowledge arise from political, economic, and cultural trajectories, shaping what is researched, funded, and legitimized. These dynamics have direct consequences for OH, as neglected areas can hinder the identification of emerging threats. It then discusses the sociology of expectations, where visions of the future operate as performative forces guiding innovation, behavior, and institutional priorities. Drawing on Luhmann's distinction between the "present future" and the "future present," the chapter argues that future-making should move beyond probability-based prediction toward the active production of possibilities and futures literacy. The final sections introduce key methodologies from sociology and future studies – scenario planning, the Delphi method, and backcasting – explaining how they enable the exploration of multiple possible futures, support anticipatory forms of decision-making, and help design flexible, adaptive strategies in complex OH contexts. By integrating sociological insights with forecasting tools, OH can shift from a reactive model of preparedness to an anticipatory approach capable of addressing uncertainty, recognizing emerging signals, and involving diverse stakeholders. Futures literacy thus becomes essential for constructing more equitable, inclusive, and sustainable health futures across interconnected human–animal–environmental systems.

Keywords: Future studies; undone science; sociology of ignorance; sociology of expectations; Delphi method; backcasting

INTRODUCTION

One of the main reasons why the OH approach is now particularly valued and promoted is its ability to predict potential ecological and pandemic disasters. This prerogative stems from OH's propensity to view reality as a complex, holistic, and interdependent system, providing an overview that allows for an earlier identification of warning signs that might be missed with a focus only on human health, animal health, or environmental issues. OH involves experts from different disciplines, including medical doctors, veterinarians, biologists, ecologists, epidemiologists, sociologists, and economists. However, there may be less awareness of *how* it is possible, within a OH paradigm, to make predictions, construct future scenarios, or identify emerging trends. In this chapter, we will be presenting the main sociological theories regarding the future and connecting them to the forecasting methodologies proposed in sociology and in the field future studies. These are methods that can make OH immediately concrete and operational.

Specifically, in the "Undone Science" section, we will be introducing the concept of "undone science," showing that there are areas of scientific research that are not studied due to social, political, and economic factors. We will then examine how this lack of research can have significant consequences for public health, social justice, and the environment.

In the "Functions of Ignorance" section, we will delve deeper into the sociology of ignorance, analyzing how ignorance – understood not only as a lack of knowledge but also as a social construct – comes about and is used in society. We will explore the causes, functions, and consequences of ignorance, highlighting how it can be used to maintain power, control information, and construct dominant scientific models.

In the "Types of Ignorance" section, we will present a typology of different forms of ignorance, including rational, strategic, pluralistic, and structured ignorance (and negative knowledge). We will also analyze how these different forms of ignorance influence individual and collective decisions, perpetuating social inequalities and ecological imbalances.

In the "Sociology of Expectations" section, we will examine the role of expectations, understood as active forces that influence the behavior, interactions, and decisions of individuals and organizations. We will also discuss how expectations regarding the future have the power to influence and shape innovation processes.

In the "The Presence (and the Present) of the Future" section, we will discuss how the future can be actualized through probability calculations and scenario building.

For a long time, the future has been made "present" through the probability calculation, assuming a line of continuity between past, present, and future. However, this approach no longer appears convincing, and "future-making" practices are shifting toward the active production of possibilities that intervene in the course of events.

In the "Techniques for Predicting the Future" section, we will present some of the main techniques for predicting the future, including scenario planning, the Delphi method, and backcasting. Specifically, we will describe how these techniques can be used to explore different possible futures, develop flexible strategies, and adapt to emerging changes in the field of OH.

UNDONE SCIENCE

"Undone science," also known as unrealized science or incomplete science, is a concept in sociology that describes areas of scientific research that are not studied due to a series of social, political, and economic factors. "Undone science" is not simply knowledge that has "not yet been discovered," but rather knowledge that is *actively* not produced, or, as demonstrated in the following section, knowledge that is *ignored*. Therefore, undone science is not merely a lack of knowledge, but a lack of research and development on certain topics. It is an active choice *not* to investigate certain areas. It inevitably follows that other areas will receive attention and funding. In these areas, discoveries will be made, and alliances will be built, and these areas will develop and become dominant and "institutionalized."

The first reason for undone science is funding. Research areas that are not considered profitable receive little funding, so scientific discoveries related to those topics will never come to light. A second cause of undone science is private interests: companies can suppress or hinder research that questions the safety or efficacy of their products. Furthermore, and this is the third factor, in some fields, research (and, therefore, also non-research) can be influenced by gender and racial bias, which means that certain groups will be under-represented in research, and that health issues specific to these groups – at least in the case of research carried out on people – will be neglected. Finally, there is a fourth factor, with a broader range than the others: social and cultural values can influence which research topics are considered "legitimate" or "important." For example, in a strongly religious and conservative society, there will not be many incentives to conduct research on reproductive health.

"Undone science" can, therefore, have significant consequences for public health, social justice, and the environment, including animals. For example, the lack of research on diseases that predominantly affect low-income populations can lead to a lack of effective treatments and policies. Again, the following three cases can be mentioned as examples:

- *Research on women's health*: Traditionally, medical research has focused on men, leading to a lesser understanding of health conditions specific to women.
- *Orphan diseases*: Rare diseases that affect a limited number of people often receive less attention in research than more common diseases.
- *Environmental impact of industrial practices*: Research into the environmental impact of certain industrial practices may be thwarted by the companies involved.

Undone science can contribute to perpetuating social inequalities because a lack of knowledge about certain issues can make it more difficult to address them effectively:

> *(P)owerful actors, generally in industry and government, benefit from the absence of research that mobilized publics and community groups would find useful for their advocacy goals. This particular type of scientific ignorance is systematically produced because of the strategic value of ignorance to public and private organizations that generate environmental and health risks. To maintain this absence, powerful groups influence public and private funding priorities. Moreover, because funding priorities and opportunities influence the priorities of a research field, the tastes of the research field become aligned with the priorities of the dominant actors. In turn, undone science can become embedded in the habitus of*

> *research fields, and researchers who do not follow the priorities of the field can become targets of suppression. (Hess, 2020, pp. 242–243)*

In summary, the concept of "undone science" invites us to critically reflect on how scientific knowledge is produced and what factors influence research priorities. Recognizing the existence of "undone science" is an important step toward promoting more equitable, inclusive, and socially responsible research.

We can, therefore, see that many issues related to OH priorities, such as the safety of meat as food or the reduction of antibiotic consumption, not to mention climate change and many issues related to environmental exploitation, can be overshadowed, strategically underestimated, obscured, and thus relegated to a footnote in scientific agendas through specific (science) policy choices.

FUNCTIONS OF IGNORANCE

Research on undone science falls within the broader field of study of the sociology of ignorance. It is striking how little attention sociologists have directed toward "what we do not know and why" (Schiebinger, 2004, p. 237; see also Mueller, 2018). Hence, it is fair to say that "we know very little about ignorance" (Croissant, 2014, p. 4). Yet debates on non-knowledge and ignorance go at least as far back as Socrates' insistence that his wisdom lay in "knowing what he did not know."

The sociology of ignorance is a field of study within sociology that analyzes how ignorance – understood not only as a lack of knowledge but also as a social construct – comes about and is used in society, and also in groups and institutions. It is an area of research that actively explores the causes, functions, and consequences of ignorance, rather than taking it for granted or simply considering it a deficit. Incidentally, it is worth remembering how popular wisdom has emphasized the functionality of ignorance in everyday life: excessive curiosity and the inclination to know are also deprecated in sayings, proverbs, and maxims from all periods and places, from "curiosity killed the cat" to "where 'tis folly to be wise, ignorance is bliss," along with "what you don't know won't hurt you" and "let sleeping dogs lie."

The sociology of ignorance is founded on the rejection of the idea that ignorance is simply a lack of objective knowledge. Consequently, sociology sees ignorance as a product of social, cultural, and political processes. Ignorance is, therefore, not a static entity, but a dynamic process that varies according to the social context and the power of those who define it. For this reason, the sociology of ignorance focuses on how ignorance is actively produced and maintained. This can be done through various strategies, including the suppression of information, the spread of misinformation, the creation of doubt, and the construction of "structured ignorance."

Structured ignorance refers to situations in which lack of knowledge is systematic and embedded in institutions, norms, and social practices. For example, companies may suppress scientific research on the health risks of their products, or governments may restrict access to information in order to maintain political control.

Furthermore, in certain cases, a lack of knowledge, that is, ignorance, is not necessary to deny the existence of a phenomenon. It may be enough to cast doubt and fuel uncertainty:

> *(T)here has been enough scientific consensus and a multiplicity of evidence since the mid-1990s to be able to state empirically that anthropogenic global warming has occurred. However, conservative think tanks have stressed the "uncertainty" of the models and the evidence. This represents a conflation of the meaning of uncertainty as a probabilistic outcome, and uncertainty meaning unknown or unreliable. (Croissant, 2014, p. 6)*

Ignorance can serve various social functions, and certainly not democratic ones. As mentioned above, ignorance can be used to maintain power and control on the part of dominant groups, limiting access to information and perpetuating ideologies that justify inequalities. Consider, for example, Orwell's novel 1984, in which one of the three core slogans of the ruling Party was "ignorance is strength," meaning that the citizens' lack of knowledge and inability to question the Party's lies is what maintains the Party's absolute control and power. By controlling information and promoting a state of ignorance, the Party kept its people weak and dependent on the Party's version of reality, making them unable to rebel and cementing the Party's strength.

Ignorance can also protect the economic or political interests of individuals or organizations, by concealing harmful or risky information. Consider, for example, the ignorance regarding the risks of smoking produced for decades by multinational tobacco companies.

A third function ignorance can serve is to strengthen group identity, creating a sense of "us" versus "them" based on a common lack of knowledge or shared misconceptions. Think of the many science fiction films in which we discover how much humans and aliens have in common, or simply, here on Earth, the discovery of similarities between "natives" and immigrants.

TYPES OF IGNORANCE

Ignorance has consequences. Clearly, a lack of accurate information can lead to poor decisions, both individual and collective, but ignorance can also make people vulnerable to exploitation, manipulation, and misinformation. Furthermore, it can perpetuate social inequalities, limiting opportunities for marginalized groups. Mueller (2018) proposes a typology in which she identifies five forms of ignorance: rational ignorance, strategic ignorance, negative knowledge, pluralistic ignorance, and structured ignorance. They are listed below, with some examples provided. We have not included structured ignorance, already described above.

Rational ignorance. Choosing not to learn something because the costs (time, effort, etc.) outweigh the perceived benefits. This can be driven by material concerns or the desire to have existing beliefs validated. For instance,

> *in racialized social systems (...) ideological ignorance also becomes a "rational" goal for dominant racial groups because it makes racial domination easier to enact and defend. (Mueller, 2018, p. 5)*

Strategic ignorance. Intentionally cultivating ignorance as a tactical advantage. This can involve denying liability, asserting expertise, or, for marginalized groups, developing a consciousness resistant to oppression by choosing not to know the world as they have been taught. To describe this type of ignorance, reference can be made to a study on the strategies of the World Bank and the International Monetary Fund, in which case strategic ignorance concerned:

> *how policy-makers at the World Bank and IMF have sought alternately to dispel and to magnify ambiguity when implementing new policies or defending the performance of established ones. Through fostering "future flexibility in interpretation," ambiguity is often used strategically by those in the best position to take advantage of the fluidity of possible interpretations of their own decisions. (McGoey, 2012, p. 11, see also Best, 2012)*

Negative knowledge. This refers to ignorance produced in order to avoid "sensitive" or "embarrassing" knowledge. In other words, those areas that are best not explored because, for example, they could reveal facts that contradict our political ideas. Introduced by Knorr Cetina (1999), negative knowledge captures knowledge

> *of the limits of knowing, of the mistakes we make in trying to know, of the things that interfere with our knowing, or what we are not interested in and do not really want to know. (Knorr Cetina, 1999, p. 63)*

In other words,

> *negative knowledge captures an awareness of the things we have no incentive or interest in knowing. (Mueller, 2018, p. 6)*

Pluralistic ignorance. This type of ignorance, which might be better called "conformist ignorance," can be illustrated by the fact that many people behave in a certain way because they believe that everyone else in the same circumstances would do the same. Scholars have also used pluralistic ignorance to make sense of contradictions between Whites' racial attitudes and behavior:

> *For example, studying racial segregation in the late 1960s, (it was found that) White Americans grossly overestimated support for racial segregation among other Whites. Moreover, even as many White respondents rejected the idea that segregation was desirable, their presumptions about Whites' broader collective conscience emboldened a willingness to rationalize racial discrimination in housing. (Mueller, 2018, p. 6)*

I believe that two further forms of ignorance can be added to those above. We could call the first form "systemic" ignorance. To understand this type of ignorance, it is useful to start with a quote from Frickel:

> *over time, different types of ignorance accumulate and combine to create complex architectures or structures of non-knowledge. (Frickel, 2014, p. 264)*

This refers to how ignorance fits into a broader system of knowledge (and ignorance) that makes this type of ignorance plausible and coherent. In this system, therefore, there may also be other types of ignorance, along with true things, resulting in the formation of an epistemology, a way of knowing the world, that is coherent and, in some ways, plausible. The main example is conspiracy theories.

The other type of ignorance is "adaptive" ignorance. An example of adaptive ignorance can be observed in all those situations in which we prefer or endeavor to ignore potential risks and dangers arising from particular conditions or phenomena. For example, it is adaptive ignorance to decide not to deepen our knowledge regarding the use of nuclear energy, how a disease spreads, the ecological issues faced by our country, the consequences of the electoral victory of a particular candidate, and so on. While this form of ignorance can be called irresponsible, it undoubtedly allows us to live our lives with less anxiety (Capuano, 2020).

Clearly, these types of ignorance overlap and contain minor logical inconsistencies, but thanks mainly to Jennifer Mueller, we have a framework that undoubtedly provides fertile terrain for empirical research and theoretical arguments.

The thing we might keep in mind is that privileging certain taken-for-granted approaches to knowledge production in the realm of health can lead to the systematic production of ignorance. This absence has tangible consequences. To stay on topic, ignorance of the interdependencies between human health, animal health and environmental health will produce short-sighted and limited policies and interventions.

SOCIOLOGY OF EXPECTATIONS

Expectations are a central area of study in the social sciences, especially economics. Rational choice and expectations theory hold that:

> *aggregate predictions are correct because individual errors are random. Therefore, predicted outcomes do not diverge systematically from the resulting market equilibrium. As a consequence, the uncertainty of the future becomes a predictable forecast, paving the way for the rational calculation of optimal choices. (Beckert, 2013, p. 221)*

From this perspective, expectations correspond to collective ideas about the future (promises, visions, and concerns) that:

> *gradually become taken for granted as if they were a self-evident statement that does not need to be justified. (Palavicino, 2016, p. 38)*

This assumption has been widely criticized. Actors often have different ideas of rationality, and there may also be calculation errors and biases.

From a sociological point of view, expectations can be considered active forces that influence the behavior, interactions, and decisions of individuals and organizations (therefore, not just as simple beliefs about the future). Expectations about the future are the result of activities taking place in the present and have the power to influence and shape innovation processes in the present by coordinating actors, opening up the imagination of new possibilities and normatively guiding behavior and attitudes. In this respect, such expectations can be defined as "performative."

As Harro van Lente (1993, p. 191) argues: "expectation statements are not only representations of something that does not (yet) exist, they do something: advising, showing direction, creating obligations." Sociology of expectations focuses specifically: "on the claims to the future that are made in science and technology, and how these (seek to) shape investment, policy frameworks and so on" (Halford & Southerton, 2023, p. 265).

In this sense, the sociology of expectations stands as a specific field of future sociology. Moreover, as "wishful enactments" of desired futures: "expectations are highly normative, they embody particular ways of thinking how society should be" (Palavicino, 2016, p. 38). For this reason, although expectations are directed toward the future, they tell us a lot about the present.

An example of the performative power of expectations is the so called self-fulfilling prophecy, a classic concept in the sociology of science, devised by Robert Merton. If enough people believe that a certain event will happen (prophecy), their behavior can contribute to that event occurring, even if it was not initially certain (self-fulfilling event). For example, if everyone expects the stock market to crash, they will start selling their shares, which will actually cause the market to crash. Or if rumors spread that a bank is in trouble, customers will withdraw their savings and the bank will effectively enter into crisis. Or, if a certain technology is expected to become dominant, resources will be invested in researching and developing it, which will increase the likelihood of that technology effectively becoming dominant.

It is important to stress that *performativity* should not be understood as a causal, unilinear process in which some statements trigger consequences in the world,

> *but rather as an evolving dynamic of mutual adjustment between statements and their associated world. In this regard, the notion of performativity also contains an ambivalence that needs to be unpacked here: it can refer to [expectations] of the future that have a concrete impact on the actions and interactions of entities involved in the innovation process – and thus performativity in*

> *the sense of making things happen – and to the fact that such [expectations,] representations and perceptions of the future, as social facts in their own right, exist insofar as they are continuously and practically enacted, indeed "performed," by social actors. (Favalli, 2024, p. 32)*

In other words, the reality of expectations "does not precede the mundane practices in which we interact with it but is rather shaped within these practices" (Mol, 1999, p. 75). Expectations and practices refer to two aspects, often difficult to distinguish, of the same process.

This complexity and uncertainty of the future require sociologists (and OH scholars) to develop new conceptual tools "to engage with the 'produced future' in progress, which is latent and invisible until it materializes as fact sometime, somewhere" (Adam, 2011, p. 594).

The main methodologies for predicting the future are presented in the "Techniques for Predicting the Future" section of this chapter.

THE PRESENCE (AND THE PRESENT) OF THE FUTURE

In the discussions so far on undone science, the sociology of ignorance and the performative power of expectations, a stone guest looms: someone, or something, still and silent, but with a huge influence on all events. Someone, or something, that is not present: an absence, yet it is as if it were present. It is the future.

We have Niklas Luhmann to thank for a conceptual distinction that forms the basis of the sociology of the future: present future and future present. The *present future* is the future as a reality perceived in the present. It is a way of describing how people engage mentally and emotionally with the future. In contrast, the *future present* is a conceptualized future, an inaccessible temporal abstraction, a point in the time continuum that is not accessible from any temporally situated perspective (Luhmann, 1976). More specifically, the *future present* is understood as a specific type of uncertainty that social systems necessarily have to deal with through the production of *present futures*. In other words:

> *The present future is the image (or images) of the future that one can have or imagine today – based on the available information. But the future present, the real future given that will become actual at a later time as yet undetermined, is different from the present*

> *future because it results from a multiplicity of factors that did not previously exist and could not be considered as information. (Esposito, 2024, p. 217)*

One way to make the future present is to calculate probabilities. Assuming that the future present is a linear extension of the past and present, we know it in its present future through the calculation and estimation of the probabilities of certain events occurring. In practice, we carry out a "defuturization," according to Luhmann's systems theory. However, this model does not seem to have much of a future.

Today, the proposed future-making practices programmatically move from an orientation toward the future guided by the calculation of probabilities to the active production of possibilities that intervene in the course of things (Amoore, 2013). In this type of approach, performativity turns from a problem into a resource: future-making practices are "performative by their very nature" (Flyverbom & Garsten, 2021, p. 1) because "they address the future explicitly as the result of present actions" (Esposito, 2024, p. 214).

The scientific study of the future has an epistemological difficulty, however. In 1961, Bertrand de Jouvenel published one of the great classics of future studies: *L'art del conjecture*. In this volume, de Jouvenel introduces the distinction between *facta* and *futura*. *Facta* refer to past events, facts, or occurrences that have already happened and are no longer open to change, while *futura* refer to futures, a realm of possibilities and potential outcomes that can be influenced by present actions. *Futura* describe the possible futures that could emerge from different courses of action. In the words of Poli:

> *The sciences deal with facts, about which data can be collected. What has not yet happened, about which no data can be collected, does not belong to science. Therefore, there is no science of the futura. When we talk about futura, we are not talking about facts but ideas, expectations, hopes and fears. (Poli, 2017, p. 22)*

It is, therefore, no coincidence that studies on the future are characterized more as a set of methodologies than as a series of rigid scientific theories. This does not detract from the epistemological strength of future studies; after all, even statistics is a science that deals with possibilities rather than facts and is formed more by methodologies than theories.

An important classification of futures was proposed by Roy Amara (1981). Amara distinguishes between possible, plausible, probable, and preferable futures. The first three types are analytical, while the fourth is clearly normative. Amara distinguishes the first three types as follows: the scope of possible futures is the broadest and covers the entire space of what could happen. It includes all possibilities, even those we do not know how to achieve and those for which we do not yet have the necessary knowledge to achieve: think of human travel to Mars, for example. Plausible futures are a restriction of possible futures: they are the category of futures that our technical and scientific knowledge would allow us to realize. Probable futures are a restriction of plausible futures: they are futures based on current trends. If we read this sequence backwards,

> *probable futures are those that are already happening around us; plausible futures are those that could happen if only we used the knowledge we have; possible futures are those that could happen by developing new knowledge. (Poli, 2017, p. 17)*

At this point, it is worth mentioning a further distinction: the "future of" and the "future in" (Poli, 2017). The former – the "future of" – regards the acquisition of technical knowledge in an attempt to understand the future, for example, of home care. In this case, we should take into account artificial intelligence, home automation, and digital applications. The future composition of families will probably also play a role: the decline in births will affect the health of elderly people living alone, as well as welfare measures, of course. As we can see, exercises of the "future of" type require specific technical skills and presuppose in-depth analysis both of the scenarios or sectors of reference and of global macro-trends.

The latter expression – "future in" – refers to the structured introduction of future skills within an organization or institution and even within communities and among individuals. It is about acquiring the ability to actively use the future in the present, that is, to develop the skills necessary to "let the future speak." In this case, the underlying skill is more cultural and attitudinal than technical, although it obviously cannot fail to include a number of technical elements. This is what we call "futures literacy" (Miller, 2010). *Futures literacy* is the ability to use the future for a better understanding of the present. It is not about predicting the future, but about using the ability to imagine different futures to understand our current assumptions, prejudices, and fears and to make more informed and conscious decisions in the present. In the context of OH, it is clear that this is an ability of enormous importance.

Furthermore, according to UNESCO (2012), since the future does not already exist but is open to being remade through the choices and actions of people living in the present, futures literacy should also be an individual skill to be learned in educational contexts. Knowing how to "use the future" should be a capability that anyone can use in their daily lives.[1]

In recent years, the OH approach has been revived and valued for the knowledge it can provide to anticipate and prevent possible (indeed, probable) pandemics. The holistic and proactive nature of OH is cited as the advantage this approach has in predicting a possible pandemic, as well as other potential negative events that must be analyzed from a broad perspective.

In this context, it is, therefore, useful to have a clearer understanding of what is meant by preparedness and anticipation. Before examining these two ways of dealing with the future, it is worth highlighting an important distinction related to the possibilities of prediction. The reliability of OH for forecasting is based on the tendency for it to be used in complex contexts. Complex systems are different from complicated systems. While both can be challenging to understand and manage, the key difference lies in the nature of their interactions, predictability, and the emergence of novel behaviors.

A complicated system is made up of many parts that interact in a predictable and linear way. The relationships between the parts are usually clearly defined and understood. Given the inputs, the outputs can be reliably predicted, because the system behaves in a consistent and repeatable manner. Linearity means that cause and effect relationships are clear and proportional. For example, a small change in input leads to a small change in output. In terms of control, it can be managed and controlled from a central point. Moreover, a complicated system is predictable. The system's behavior is simply the sum of the behavior of its parts. No unexpected behaviors arise. An example of a complicated system could be a computer program: it has many lines of code, but operates according to deterministic rules.

On the other hand, a complex system is a system composed of many interconnected and interdependent parts that interact in non-linear and unpredictable ways. The relationships between the parts are dynamic and can change over time. The system's behavior is impossible to predict with certainty. Small changes in initial conditions can lead to large and unexpected outcomes (the "butterfly effect"). Indeed, cause and effect relationships are often disproportionate and difficult to trace (non-linearity), and unexpected behaviors or properties can arise from the interactions of the parts. The system as a whole exhibits properties that are not present in its individual components, and understanding the parts does not necessarily lead to understanding the whole. It is not surprising that the example of a complex system that is usually given is the ecosystem. Other examples are the city (a complex web of social, economic, and political interactions) and the stock market (which is influenced by a multitude of economic factors and human emotions).

Nowadays, many problems

> *are made worse by trading one type of problem for the other, because the problems arising from what makes a system complicated can eventually be solved, while those arising from what makes a system complex can at best be transformed or modified, but not solved once and for all. (Poli, 2015, p. 94)*

Broadly speaking, anticipation refers to the act of predicting, imagining, or exploring potential futures. It is a proactive process of recognizing trends, possibilities, and risks, aimed at developing future scenarios or visions. Preparedness, on the other hand, regards the ability to respond effectively to foreseeable future events, risks, or crises. It is the process of planning, strengthening capabilities, and creating strategies to effectively address the potential challenges identified through anticipation. In summary, and again broadly speaking, anticipation is the process of predicting and imagining possible futures, while preparedness consists of organization and preparation to effectively address them. In other words, anticipation is about knowing what might happen, while preparedness is about being ready to handle what might happen. The two are complementary: anticipation helps in seeing potential futures, while preparedness ensures control over future uncertainties.

In Futures Studies, however, this distinction is not so clear-cut, and we know from the sociology of ignorance and the performative version of expectation theory that it is not always possible to keep the dimensions of anticipation and preparedness separate. After all,

> *A system behaving in an anticipatory way – an anticipatory system – takes its decisions in the present according to "anticipations" about something that may eventually happen in the future. (Poli, 2015, p. 97)*

Through anticipation, we integrate the future into the present and make decisions based on this presentification of the future, so our decisions, in part, prepare us for the future.

The distinction between forecast and foresight plays an important role, too. In short, forecasts regard extrapolation from data, while foresight regards the visualization of possible futures. The difference lies in the way the future is made explicit: in the case of forecasting, the future is constructed as a repetition of past patterns, while in the case of foresight, the future also contains genuine innovations and discontinuities. We could say that in the case of forecasting, we attempt to predict the most likely future; in the case of foresight, we scientifically construct multiple possible futures. However, in research practice, it is not always possible to keep these dimensions clearly distinct. There is also confusion in the use of terms within future studies itself. Nevertheless, it is important to have a clear grasp of this analytical dimension. In discussing methodologies, we will, therefore, use the terms with reference to the context in which they were conceived, putting Poli's important analytical distinction in brackets.

TECHNIQUES FOR PREDICTING THE FUTURE

In this section, we present some of the main techniques for predicting the future: scenario planning, the Delphi method, and backcasting methodology. This is obviously a subjective choice, and the list could be longer. To gain an in-depth understanding of – and possibly learn how to use – future forecasting techniques in practice, it is advisable to refer to specialist texts.

Scenario Planning

Scenario planning is a strategic tool that helps organizations prepare for potential future changes by exploring and analyzing a range of possible futures. The process involves defining the scope and identifying key driving forces and uncertainties, developing plausible scenarios based on these factors, and then creating strategic responses to navigate each scenario.

To summarize Ringland (2003), it generally works as follows:

1. *Definition of the objective*: the problem or decision to be addressed is established, along with the context in which planning is desired.
2. *Identification of key variables*: the most influential and uncertain elements that may affect the future are identified (e.g., economic, political, social, technological factors).
3. *Collection of weak signals and trends*: an analysis is conducted of signs of change and current trends, for a better understanding of possible futures.
4. *Creation of scenarios*: several plausible scenarios, usually 3–4, are built, combining various levels of uncertainty and trends. These scenarios represent different alternative worlds, such as an optimistic scenario, a pessimistic scenario, and an intermediate scenario.

5. *Scenario analysis*: the implications of each scenario are examined, identifying opportunities and threats and developing flexible and resilient strategies.

6. *Use and monitoring*: the strategies developed are put into practice and the context is constantly monitored to update scenarios and plans, adapting them to emerging changes.

In summary, scenario planning helps to imagine different possible futures and to prepare for them more effectively, developing adaptability and strategic flexibility.

The Delphi Method

The Delphi method is a structured research technique for the purpose of obtaining consensus on a specific issue from a selected group of experts. Its main distinguishing features are anonymity, an iterative multi-cycle process and the presence of controlled feedback (Maturo, 1999). In practice, questions are e-mailed to experts and the responses are collected and anonymously sent back to all the experts, who then have the opportunity to modify their views. Several rounds of this type are carried out. This method is particularly useful for addressing complex or uncertain issues, such as the formulation of public policies, the analysis of trends, or the prediction of future scenarios, where historical information is insufficient for accurate forecasting.

The process consists of the following stages:

1. *Selection of the panel of experts*: A group of experts in the field of interest is identified. It is crucial for the panel to be both competent and representative of multiple viewpoints.

2. *First round of questionnaires*: The coordinator sends a first questionnaire open to all the experts, asking them to freely express their opinions and predictions on the topic under consideration.

3. *Analysis and synthesis*: The coordinator collects and analyzes the responses from the first round, identifying points of agreement and disagreement and summarizing the various reasons.

4. *Subsequent rounds*: The summarized responses are sent back to the experts in a subsequent questionnaire. Each expert can review their position in light of the responses of the others, while maintaining anonymity. This process is repeated for several rounds, until the group's

responses show a sufficiently high degree of convergence, or until the responses stabilize.

5. *Final result*: At the end of the process, the coordinator prepares a final report summarizing the converging opinions of the panel of experts, providing a consensus or an overview of the different positions.

Because it is based on anonymity, the Delphi method eliminates psychological barriers and group influences, such as conformity or pressure from a dominant opinion, encouraging more sincere and independent expression from each expert. The validity of the results depends directly on the competence and diversity of the experts chosen. A non-representative or insufficiently competent panel can negatively impact the reliability of the conclusions (Maturo, 1999).

The Backcasting Methodology

Backcasting is a strategic planning methodology that starts from a vision of the desired future and works backward to define the steps and actions necessary to achieve it (Bibri, 2018). Unlike forecasting, which projects the future based on the past, backcasting does not focus on prediction, but on actively constructing the future. The goal is to connect the present to the desired (or undesired) future by identifying the decisions and actions that need to be taken at each stage.

The process takes place in several stages:

1. *Definition of the future vision*: A clear vision of a desirable long-term future (e.g., in 25–50 years) is established. This vision can be very specific and include measurable objectives.

2. *Scenario analysis*: The conditions that must be met for the vision to become a reality are described, identifying technological, social, and economic factors.

3. *Identification of pathways*: Working backward from the desired future, the key milestones, necessary changes, and obstacles to be overcome in order to bridge the gap between the current situation and the final goal are identified.

4. *Development of an action plan*: A detailed plan is created that defines the concrete actions and responsibilities for the various actors involved, in order to move from the present towards the established future.

Backcasting is a normative method, because it focuses on what the future should be, rather than just predicting what it might be. We might say that it goes "back to the future!"

OH AND THE FUTURE

As we have seen, sociology and future studies offer a range of tools and methods that can enrich and enhance the OH approach, helping to predict emerging health threats, assess environmental impacts, plan integrated strategies, promote innovation, and engage various types of stakeholders.

With regard to anticipating health threats, the connection between forecasting methodologies and OH can address emerging health threats, such as new zoonoses or the evolution of antibiotic resistance. Specifically, sociology and future studies provide us with the tools to analyze global trends, such as climate change, population growth, urbanization, and economic transformations. As demonstrated by OH, these trends have a direct impact on human, animal, and environmental health and can increase the risk of zoonoses, antibiotic resistance, and other health crises. For example, analyzing demographic trends can help us understand how population growth and increased population density in certain geographical areas can facilitate the spread of infectious diseases. The study of climate change can reveal how rising temperatures and changes in precipitation patterns can alter the geographical distribution of disease vectors, such as mosquitoes and ticks, and thus increase the risk of transmission of diseases to humans and animals. We should not overlook the fact that the flexibility of forecasting methodologies allows for rapid, just-in-time research to be carried out when unexpected events occur and their consequences need to be assessed quickly.

Along these lines, future studies can facilitate the planning of integrated strategies that address complex health challenges holistically, in line with the OH philosophy. It is, therefore, a question of using sociological methodologies to construct and explore possible futures. This is the basis for developing flexible action plans that take into account the interconnections between human, animal, and environmental health. This can only happen by involving a wide range of stakeholders, including scientists, politicians, healthcare professionals, farmers, and local communities, in the forecasting and planning process. Recognizing that different stakeholders may have different perspectives on the future, sociology and future studies increasingly emphasizes participatory and critical approaches that involve a wide range of voices in the process of envisioning and shaping the future. However, the participatory aspect of OH is not limited to the conception and imagination of the future, nor is it limited to the inclusion of "expert stakeholders." On the contrary, social participation and community involvement are a priority aspect of the OH approach, as we will see in the next chapter.

Last but not least, sociology and future studies can stimulate innovation in the field of OH by encouraging the development of new technologies, approaches, and policies to address emerging health challenges. Through the analysis of technological trends and the exploration of future scenarios, it is possible to identify the areas where innovation can have the greatest impact.

NOTE

1. See https://www.unesco.org/en/futures-literacy/about

REFERENCES

Adam, B. (2011). Wendell Bell and the sociology of the future: Challenges past, present and future. *Futures*, *43*(6), 590–595. https://doi.org/10.1016/j.futures.2011.04.007

Amara, R. (1981). Views on futures research methodology. *Futures*, *23*(6), 645–649. https://doi.org/10.1016/0016-3287(91)90085-G

Amoore, L. (2013). *The politics of possibility. Risk and security beyond probability*. Duke University Press.

Beckert, J. (2013). Imagined futures: Fictional expectations in the economy. *Theory and Society*, *42*(3), 219–240. https://doi.org/10.1007/s11186-013-9191-2

Best, J. (2012). Bureaucratic ambiguity. *Economy and Society*, *41*(1), 84–106. https://doi.org/10.1080/03085147.2011.637333

Bibri, S. E. (2018). Backcasting in futures studies: A synthesized scholarly and planning approach to strategic smart sustainable city development. *European Journal of Futures Research*, 6(13), 2–27. https://doi.org/10.1186/s40309-018-0142-z

Capuano, R. G. (2020). Introduzione. In W. E. Moore & M. M. Toumin (2020, o.v. 1949). (a cura di), *Alcune funzioni sociali dell'ignoranza*. Armando Editore.

Croissant, J. L. (2014). Agnotology: Ignorance and absence or towards a sociology of things that aren't there. *Social Epistemology*, *28*(1), 4–25. https://doi.org/10.1080/02691728.2013.862880

Esposito, E. (2024). Can we use the open future? Preparedness and innovation in times of self-generated uncertainty. *European Journal of Social Theory*, 27(2), 209–224. https://doi.org/10.1177/13684310231224546

Favalli, R. (2024). *Following the futures of an emerging technology: The case of brain-computer interfaces* (Tesi di dottorato, Università degli Studi di Padova). Deposito istituzionale. https://www.research.unipd.it/bitstream/11577/3520303/2/tesi_Roberto_Favalli.pdf

Flyverbom, M., & Garsten, C. (2021). Anticipation and organization: Seeing, knowing and governing futures. *Organization Theory*, 2, 1–25. https://doi.org/10.1177/26317877211020325

Frickel, S. (2014). Not here and everywhere: The non-knowledge of science. In D. L. Kleinman & K. Moore (Eds.), *Routledge handbook of science, technology, and society* (pp. 263–276). Routledge.

Halford, S., & Southerton, D. (2023). What future for the sociology of futures? Visions, concepts and methods. *Sociology*, *57*(2), 263–278. https://doi.org/10.1177/00380385231157586

Hess, J. D. (2020). The sociology of ignorance and post-truth politics. *Sociological Forum*, *35*(1), 241–249. https://doi.org/10.1111/socf.12577

Knorr Cetina, K. (1999). *Epistemic cultures: How the sciences make knowledge*. Harvard University Press.

Luhmann, N. (1976). The future cannot begin: Temporal structures in modern society. *Social Research*, *43*(1), 130–152.

Maturo, A. (1999). Una ricerca sul lavoratore post-industriale e il futuro del lavoro: l'uso della tecnica Delphi. In M. La Rosa (a cura di), *Problemi del lavoro e strategie di ricerca empirica*. Milano.

McGoey, L. (2012). Strategic unknowns: Towards a sociology of ignorance. *Economy and Society*, *41*(1), 1–16. https://doi.org/10.1080/03085147.2011.637330

Miller, R. (2010). Futures literacy – Embracing complexity and using the future. *Ethos*, *10*(10), 23–28.

Mol, A. (1999). Ontological politics. A word and some questions. *The Sociological Review*, *47*(1), 74–89. https://doi.org/10.1111/j.1467-954X.1999.tb03483.x

Mueller, J. (2018). Advancing a sociology of ignorance in the study of racism and racial non-knowing. *Sociology Compass*, *12*, e12600. https://doi.org/10.1111/soc4.12600

Palavicino, C. A. (2016). *Mindful anticipation. A practice approach to the study of expectations in emerging technologies* [PhD dissertation]. University of Twente.

Poli, R. (2015). Mastering social foresight – Introduction to the special issue. *On the Horizon*, *23*(2), 81–84. https://doi.org/10.1108/OTH-02-2015-0005

Poli, R. (2017). Recuperare il senso del future. In R. Poli (a cura di). *Strategie di futuro in classe*. Trento.

Ringland, G. (2003). Scenario planning: Persuading operating managers to take ownership. *Strategy and Leadership*, *31*(6), 22–28. https://doi.org/10.1108/10878570310505569

Schiebinger, L. (2004). Feminist history of colonial science. *Hypatia*, *19*(1), 233–254.

UNESCO (2012). *What is futures literacy (FL)?* https://www.unesco.org/en/futures-literacy/about

van Lente, H. (1993). *Promising technology: The dynamics of expectations in technological developments*. University of Twente.

4

SOCIOLOGICAL THEORIES FOR ONE HEALTH

ABSTRACT

This chapter explores a set of influential sociological theories in order to demonstrate their relevance for understanding health within the One Health (OH) paradigm. Beginning with approaches to health inequalities, the text contrasts deficit explanations with structural perspectives that highlight how socio-economic disadvantage shapes exposure to adverse health outcomes. The discussion then turns to the critical tradition, examining Ivan Illich's analysis of iatrogenesis and Paul Farmer's notion of structural violence, both of which illuminate how systemic arrangements and power asymmetries constrain agency and generate avoidable suffering. These insights are complemented by micro sociological contributions, including the study of stigma and the social construction of illness, which clarify how cultural meanings, moral judgments, and patterns of interaction influence experiences of disease and environmental risk. Finally, the chapter introduces Gregory Bateson's Ecology of Mind, a systemic epistemology that challenges linear, purpose-driven models of action and encourages reframing human–environment interactions in holistic, relational terms. Together, these theories provide conceptual and methodological tools for investigating the intertwined determinants of human, animal, and ecological well-being within OH, supporting interventions sensitive to cultural contexts, social structures, and the cognitive frames through which communities interpret and respond to health challenges.

Keywords: One Health; health inequalities; structural violence; social construction of health; iatrogenesis; ecology of mind

INTRODUCTION

This chapter introduces the main theories of the sociology of healthcare. Each of these can be applied in the OH approach. We will begin by describing a number of perspectives related to health inequalities, using them as a basis on which to elaborate on the critical approach to health. In close continuity with this view, we will then introduce the concept of structural violence proposed by Paul Farmer, moving on from there to illustrate the link between social stigma and illness. The social stigma approach will subsequently be absorbed into the broader theoretical perspective of the social construction of health. We will conclude with Gregory Bateson's ecology of the mind, which is admittedly not widely practiced in the sociology of health, but is certainly connected with the epistemology of OH. Indeed, in a number of cases, the approaches proposed overlap with one another. In addition, these perspectives differ widely in terms of theoretical breadth. For example, the concept of structural violence could be seen as an aspect of critical health theory, and the same could be said of stigma and of social construction theory. However, it seems to us that by maintaining a certain analytical level, connections on OH can be more easily found. The last paragraph offers examples of the application of health sociology concepts with the OH perspective. The idea, however, is that this set of theories can be used above all as a practical and operational toolbox, depending on the circumstances of research and intervention.

SOCIOLOGICAL THEORIES ON HEALTH INEQUALITIES

In Sweden, life expectancy at birth is 83 years, while in Chad, it is 30 years less. A child born in 2021 in Treviso, Northern Italy, will live three and a half years longer than a child born in Siracusa, Sicily, in the same year. In almost every country in the world, as income rises, the smoking rate decreases. Excess weight and obesity are linked to social status, increasing the further down the social ladder we go.

We could continue with the statistics, but the trend remains stable. The social sciences are generally characterized by rather uncertain, probabilistic, and context-specific theories, while the link between health and socio-economic factors is an unassailable certainty. Income and education are linked to specific lifestyles that have consequences for health. It would be tempting to say that if less educated people smoke more and are at greater risk of obesity than university graduates, then there is an information problem, and health communication should, therefore, be enhanced for certain categories of people. This is not the case. While the relationship between social factors and health is complex, the result is unequivocal: it is the poor, the vulnerable, the "worse off" who lose out.

It is not a question of lack of information: living conditions, stress, deprivation, and uncertainty "conspire" with each other, reinforce each other, and pave the way for adverse outcomes in terms of suffering, morbidity, and mortality. This conspiracy is in plain sight, but we fail to notice the things we take for granted. Rather like Edgar Allan Poe's purloined letter.

Another aspect is that being poor is very expensive. In the United States, three rolls of toilet paper bought separately cost the same as a pack of 10, but those struggling with money buy 1 at a time. People living in poor urban areas also do not have the material opportunity to buy fresh fruit, only junk food. This is what is effectively called a "food desert." Ironically, the consolation is that even if fruit were readily available, it would be too expensive for most residents. There is no need to look at the most unequal rich country in the world, however; certain things can also be observed in Italy. For example, not everyone knows that paying a bill at a tobacconist's costs €2.50. For many people, debiting their current account is risky because they risk going into the red. So, there are huge additional costs precisely because of poverty. Not to mention access to mortgages and related interest rates, which rise in direct proportion to need. In short, although it's something of a tasteless joke, it's fair to say that the poor have expenses that the rich cannot afford.

In sociology, there are at least two important theories concerning health inequalities. Both are a far cry from the "deficit model," that is, the psychological theory that assumes health inequalities are the result of the poor being uninformed about healthy choices.

The first theory is related to the "status syndrome." This approach focuses on the effects of relative deprivation, and therefore, on the stress and unease people experience when they perceive themselves to be in lower social positions than others. According to this approach, the social position a person occupies at work influences his or her perception of exercising control over his or her life. The further down the "social hierarchy," the more a sense of helplessness and fatalism grows, and thus the conviction of being unable to control events, a skill that in psychology is called "mastery" or self-efficacy. Psychology has shown that people with a high sense of control over events, compared to those who feel at the mercy of accidents, have a higher level of health literacy, are more inclined to engage in healthy lifestyles, have a generally positive perception of their health status, fall ill less, and have a lower mortality rate.

The second theory, highly credited in sociology, is the one that refers to the "causes of causes." This approach emphasizes the effects of income and education on the other "determinants" of health. For example, people with a high level of income and education will find it easy to lead healthy lifestyles and associate with similar people, thus amplifying a virtuous circle of good health. And if and when necessary, they know how to navigate the health bureaucracy and can easily activate social connections to access information about the services they need. In contrast, people of low socio-economic status are exposed to elevated health risks. They often do not have enough money to eat healthily and turn to tobacco to alleviate monotonous or stressful work situations. Here again, social contacts are "homophilic": we tend to associate with people similar to us, who reinforce certain harmful behaviors, resulting in a vicious circle. As John Mirowski of the University of Texas effectively summarizes:

> *The poor have to bear a triple burden: they have more problems to solve; their personal histories leave them exhausted and powerless; this sense of powerlessness demoralises them and undermines their ability to take concrete action to solve problems. The result, for many, is a multiplication of illness and despair. (Mirowski, 2000, p. 53)*

It is not easy for the state to reduce health inequalities, and it is clearly very difficult to act instantly on the determinants of health. Politics seems not to be doing enough, but to be honest, in this situation of crisis of ideas, perhaps health could be a strong incentive for parties. Every family knows what it means to have a sick person at home, or indeed more than one. If politics would (finally) realize that taking care of health pays off in electoral terms, the systematic fight against health inequalities could become a reality.

THE CRITICAL APPROACH

The critical, or radical, approach, predominantly of Marxist origin, assumes the existence of a conflict between the demands of the different social classes and is oriented toward social change, that is, toward transforming the status quo. Specifically, in the sociology of health, this approach focuses on health inequalities, seen as a more or less direct emanation of economic and social inequality.

A critical approach undoubtedly underlies Ivan Illich's proposals, which, though dated, can nevertheless still offer some useful suggestions for today. Despite recognizing their significance, he does not place social inequalities at the center of his analysis.

In the 1973 volume, *Medical nemesis. The expropriation of health*, at the start of the Introduction, Illich writes:

> *The medical establishment has become a major threat to health. The disabling impact of professional control over medicine has reached the proportions of an epidemic. The name of this new epidemic, iatrogenesis, comes from iatros, the Greek word for "physician," and genesis, meaning "origin." (Illich, 1973, p. 11)*

For Illich, the medical monopoly on treatment and definitions of illness, sick, and normality has "dispossessed" man of his health. Medicine causes malfunctions in people, creeping into areas of life that once did not belong to it, and colonizing subject areas that were once independent from it:

> *Society has transferred to physicians the exclusive right to determine what constitutes sickness, who is or might become sick, and what shall be done to such people. (Illich, 1973, p. 13)*

Illich distinguishes three types of iatrogenesis:

1. clinical iatrogenesis;
2. social iatrogenesis;
3. cultural iatrogenesis.

Clinical iatrogenesis. In describing the first type of iatrogenesis, Illich starts from the observation that the predominant factors in maintaining the health of a population are environment, nutrition, hygiene, and social equality, while specifically medical intervention never appears to be significantly linked to a decrease in overall morbidity or an increase in life expectancy. On the contrary, it is precisely medical interventions, drugs, and hospitalization that produce a multitude of illnesses and damage in people. Among the negative effects (nocebo effect), Illich lists and documents numerous cases of *malpractice*, to which he adds the stimulus that drugs induce in the body to produce drug-resistant bacterial species; accidents occurring inside hospitals; and infections contracted during hospitalization. The serialization and the technicality of what were once called "the art of medicine" are the underlying causes of malpractice. In modern medicine, the errors of the physician-individual are transferred to the technological system, with the consequence that there is neither blame nor guilt: there are, at most, "percentages of error," as Illich prophetically argued in 1973. It is not difficult here to identify aspects that can be linked to OH.

Social iatrogenesis. With this term, Illich refers to the failures produced in people's health by the particular social organization of medicine. It does not refer to harm directly caused by medical doctors, drugs, and therapies, but harm indirectly caused by the health bureaucracy, the induction of new needs, and the labeling and classification of people implemented by health organizations. In part, therefore, it is the *medicalization of life*:

> *Social iatrogenesis is at work when health care is turned into a standardized item, a staple; when all suffering is "hospitalized" and homes become inhospitable to birth, sickness, and death; when the language in which people could experience their bodies is turned into bureaucratic gobbledegook; or when suffering, mourning, and healing outside the patient role are labelled a form of deviance. (Illich, 1973, p. 48)*

In affluent societies, says Illich, the doctor has to deal with two types of "addicts": those to whom he prescribes drugs and those who suffer from the consequences of drugs. Again, "permanent medical supervision" and "diagnostic imperialism" make our entire lives a series of "risk episodes," each requiring special medical protection. Illich does not spare prevention either, accusing it of being "health care" and of being "medicalized." In effect, this aspect is highly relevant today.

Cultural iatrogenesis. Cultural iatrogenesis is explained by the Austrian scholar with reference to the suppression of pain, the "invention" of illness, and the end of "natural" death. The experience of pain is not only a subjective fact but also a cultural one. There are cultures that "feel" more pain and others less; just as there are cultures in which types of pain exist that do not in others. Moreover, in many cultures, pain is regarded as natural and as a part of life (e.g., in the case of illness). Culture, therefore, gives form and intensity to physical pain. An example of how pain is today seen as a disease in itself is the phenomenon of painkiller abuse in the United States. The "opioid crisis" refers precisely to the huge number of addicts created by the use of perfectly legal painkillers. These people often moved on to using Fentanyl, a very powerful analgesic, about 50 times more powerful than morphine. This drug has led to the deaths of tens of thousands of young people in the United States.

The question is indubitably complex, and sometimes, Illich's discourse is more suggestive than realistic. We know how important the use of pain medication is in the case of cancer. In Italy, the use of opioids for cancer pain was subject to stringent regulations, leading to inadequate pain management in many patients. It was not until 2010, thanks to a new law, that access to opioid drugs for cancer patients improved.

These three types of iatrogenesis illustrate how, in Illich's view, disease is seen as an invention created to avoid questioning the legitimacy of the social order and that many illnesses are the effect of an oppressive social order:

> *People would rebel if medicine did not explain their biological disorientation as a defect in their health, rather than as a defect in the way of life which is imposed on them or which they impose on themselves. (Illich, 1973, p. 170)*

Disease, and no longer man, becomes the center of the medical system. This substitution is implemented through measurements, experiments, and evaluations based on technical standards.

> *The use of physical measurements prepared for a belief in the real existence of diseases and their ontological autonomy from the perception of doctor and patient. The use of statistics underpinned this belief. It "showed" that diseases were present in the environment and could invade and infect people. (Illich, 1973, p. 165)*

In short, making the problem of disease coincide with people's biology and physiology strengthens the power of medicine, inducing us to look at the finger rather than the moon. If we fail to understand that pollution, inadequate nutrition (today we would say junk food) and zoonoses caused by urbanization are the causes of disease, we will continue to legitimize and to perpetuate an oppressive social order.

Another important version of the critical approach is the Political Economy of Health Perspective. This theory focuses on how modes of organizing (or diz-organizing) economic actions and power structures influence population health outcomes and access to care. For example, a central theme of analysis in the Political Economy of Health Perspective is the impact of trade agreements, funding flows and economic policies on health systems and on individuals. Other scholars have devoted their efforts to evaluating how privatization, neoliberal policies, and resource allocation affect the structure and efficacy of health systems. A particularly original voice is that of Paul Farmer. Farmer (2005) provided a clear, incisive description of the mechanism of "structural violence," that is, how anonymous systemic mechanisms – decided, however, by someone in the highest spheres of power – are a death sentence for people from the most vulnerable groups. Farmer presents his theory not only with arguments but also with actual cases he witnessed when working as a doctor in Haiti in the 1980s.

STRUCTURAL VIOLENCE

Paul Farmer shows the ways in which the social matrix the individual is embedded in conditions, or rather determines, his or her destiny, and specifically how economic, cultural, and social factors structure people's suffering and pain. So, the question underlying his research in the field is:

> *By what mechanisms do social forces ranging from poverty to racism become embodied as individual experience? (Farmer, 2005, p. 266)*

This is also his understanding of the concept of "structural violence." In his famous work *Pathologies of Power* (2005), he tells the story of one of his patients, Acephie Joseph. This girl's fate is sealed from the outset by an environmental disaster involving her family and her community.

It is the 1980s, in Haiti, one of the poorest and most violent countries in the world. Acephie is 19 years old, lives with her family, and is still at primary school. Acephie's family is very poor. They are part of the "water people," a large group of people living in Kay, a refugee settlement. A few years earlier, their thriving village was washed away by water, and they had to move to stony hillsides due to the construction of a huge dam: "a project conceived in the Haitian capital and drafted in Washington DC" (Farmer, 2005, p. 270).

Before the dam, they lived a perfectly decent life on land that produced abundant harvests. The flood swept away both their homes and the graves of their ancestors.

Acephie's family became increasingly poverty-stricken, and she had to try to find a job. One day, while she was with her mother at the market, an hour and a half's walk away, some soldiers began what we would now call "catcalling": vulgar, taunting remarks addressed toward women.

> *Such flirtation is seldom rejected, at least openly. In rural Haiti, entrenched poverty made the soldiers – the region's only salaried*

> *men – ever so much more attractive. Hunger was a near-daily occurrence for the Joseph family; the times were as bad as those right after the flooding of the valley. And so when Acephie's good looks caught the eye of Captain Jacques Honorat, […] she returned his gaze. (Farmer, 2005, p. 272)*

And so, Acephie and Honorat had an affair, although he was married. No one had anything to say to her, although the village elders were not at all happy about it. However, their affair was short-lived. He fell ill and returned to live with his wife. Acephie was shocked to learn that he died shortly afterward. But she did not lose heart. She moved to Port au Prince, where she found work as a maid for a wealthy family. It was a good job, which exceeded her expectations. After a while, she also found a young man, Blanco, also from Kay, who was working as a driver and making good money. They became engaged and were planning to marry. Acephie fell pregnant. Blanco was not thrilled at the news, and the lady Acephie worked for even less so at the idea of a maid with a baby bump. Acephie had no choice but to return to her parents. Her relationship with Blanco ended. Acephie gave birth to a daughter, and was diagnosed with Aids. The few months she lived with her daughter were miserable due to diarrhea and persistent weakness. In the village, she was said to be a victim of witchcraft. She died shortly afterward. Acephie's twin brother and their mother were overcome with grief, but few realized the desperation of her father, who later hanged himself. Acephie was not the only victim, however. Earlier, there had been Captain Honorat, who infected her. Then, his wife and two of his five children. Then, another soldier with whom Honorat's wife had a relationship after his death. His wife found herself destitute, and with five children to support, she considered herself lucky to have found another soldier. And, there was also another woman Honorat had an affair with that was HIV-positive. And what about Blanco? Good-looking and – by Haiti's modest standards – a good catch, he attracted plenty of girls…

Now, who is to blame for Acephie's death? Captain Honorat, of course, is the one who infected her. But are there other characters with a direct or indirect role? If Acephie had had more financial and cultural resources, would she have accepted the captain's advances? If the water refugees had had more money, perhaps they could have gone to the market by car instead of walking past the soldiers' post. And if Acephie had had a higher level of education, she could have found a job that afforded her more protection. And her father might have been more "resilient" had he not been tested by a life marked by poverty and stress.

Paul Farmer has no doubts. Acephie is a victim of structural violence, which creates death, pain, and suffering:

> *The term is apt because such suffering is "structured" by historically given (and often economically driven) processes and forces that conspire – whether through routine, ritual, or, as is more commonly the case, the hard surfaces of life – to constrain agency. For many, including most of my patients and informants, choices both large and small are limited by racism, sexism, political violence, and grinding poverty. (Farmer, 2005, pp. 280–281)*

Thus, context shapes the course of people's lives (and deaths). Honorat is simply the personification of a set of lethal factors that interacted to drive Acephie toward her destiny. Those factors are (poor) education, poverty, sexism, social discrimination, and violence. In short, the miserable conditions the refugees were living in because of the dam: a work decided by faceless economic forces. These forces are systemic, so it is tempting to say that they have neither eyes to see the – indirect yet terrible – consequences of their actions, nor a conscience to mourn them. In summary, Farmer's approach is multi-layered:

> *to explain suffering, one must embed individual biography in the larger matrix of culture, history, and political economy. (Farmer, 2005, p. 281)*

SOCIAL STIGMA

The favorite sociologist with students is probably Erving Goffman. Goffman's works are written clearly and fluently. Most importantly, since Goffman focuses his attention on face-to-face relationships, his sociological arguments are immediately verifiable in everyday life.

Erving Goffman's sociological theory is described as "dramaturgical" because it conceives people as "social actors" engaged in a performance. In the course of social relations, we are constantly striving to maintain a common "definition of the situation," and Goffman lists and describes how, together, social actors try to contain awkward moments, potential conflicts, and being "out of face."

He has provided numerous insights for anyone dealing with the sociology of health and illness, paying particularly close attention to mental illness, to how society "treats" people with stigma, especially in "total institutions" (such as asylums).

In *Stigma*, Goffman analyzes the social condition of people with "socially undesirable" diversity (Goffman, 1963). In ancient Greece, the word "stigma" referred to the marks that were engraved – with a knife or a hot blade – on someone's body to indicate that he or she was a slave, a traitor or a person who had committed some wrongdoing. In this sense, we could equate "stigma" with the bell worn by lepers in the Middle Ages, or the cross of David drawn on the shops of Jews during Nazism.

According to Goffman, an individual carrying a stigma is condemned to "disrupt" interactions, to a greater or lesser extent. Elements liable to perturb interaction, which we should have the delicacy to "not notice," include not only physical defects:

> *Persons with a social stigma of a racial or ethnic kind, and those with a moral stigma, such as ex-mental patients, ex-convicts, and homosexuals, also share this predicament. Such individuals must learn to deal with the unhappy property of being inimical to almost every encounter in which they see themselves. (Goffman, 1963, p. 59)*

Goffman gives many accounts of blind people and people with other disabilities, to show how, in social relationships, diversity triggers reactions that would not have occurred if everyone in the relationship had been "normal." In some cases, the other social actors involved in the communication may have "negative" reactions, such as sneering or teasing; however,

> *in most cases, [the stigmatized individual] will find that there are sympathetic others who are ready to adopt his standpoint in the world and share with him the feeling that he is human and "essentially" normal in spite of appearances and in spite of his own self-doubts. (Goffman, 1959, p. 23)*

Finally, it may happen that the stigmatized person is treated as a "nonperson." Goffman's concept of nonperson dates back to 1959, four years before the publication of *Stigma*, and can be found in *Everyday Life as Representation*: nonpersons are those generic categories of people who

> *although present, are considered as if they were not there; the most common examples are the very young, the old and the sick. (Goffman, 1959, p. 177)*

Although Goffman's writing style is undoubtedly open to criticism today, we must remember that his most important works were published in the

1950s and 1960s, prior to the advent of the political correctness debate. Nonetheless, a certain cynicism can be noted in his arguments, especially when he refers to the balance of social relationships, regardless of the people who are part of them.

Scambler and Hopkins (1986) suggest splitting the concept of stigma into enacted stigma and perceived stigma. Enacted stigma refers to the perception of an action directed toward individuals with a stigmatizing trait; perceived stigma refers to the state of embarrassment and shame an individual feels about their stigmatizing condition. This distinction makes it possible to distinguish between behavior toward certain people and their feelings about their condition.

On this very distinction, Scavarda (2021) conducted research on parents of children with Down syndrome and parents of autistic children. Interviews with parents of autistic children show that, on the one hand, they perceive feelings of pity and politeness in their regard, and on the other hand, they are implicitly "blamed" for their inability to practice intensive parenting and thus to bring up their child properly. They also report experiences of hostile stares, social distancing, and even disrespectful comments.

The "courtesy stigma" is strongly perceived by parents of children with Down syndrome, who are often treated with cloying pity. So, having children with cognitive disabilities can, in some cases, be a sign of "moral blame" – at least on the part of strangers. Not surprisingly, it is mothers who are stigmatized, much more than fathers. However, mothers of children with Down syndrome are also stigmatized. In this case, they are considered "guilty" of not having had the tests that can predict the syndrome done.

In both cases, mothers react by saying that their children lead "normal" lives anyway. In the case of autistic children, it is said that they are basically like their peers. This "normalization" is also applied to children with Down syndrome, with some parents emphasizing that theirs was a "conscious choice." Again, in both cases, Scavarda reports how, in order to counter the "tragic narrative," parents use a very sophisticated vocabulary to criticize the classical biomedical view of disability and to advocate a social model of disability, even questioning the very existence of disability (Scavarda, 2021).

Stigma has provided the impetus for numerous studies on *labelling*, that is, the way socially constructed meanings regarding certain categories of people (immigrants, the mentally ill) slip into institutional and common-sense domains and then act as self-fulfilling prophecies (e.g., being an immigrant as an "explanation" for deviant behavior).

Goffman's studies on stigma can be considered a foundation for a variety of research works in the sociology of health. First and foremost, they can provide us with indications for possible investigations into the social status of HIV-positive people, or of those with disabilities. Second (but no less importantly), there are those who do not have a visible stigma, but whom prejudice constructs as a potential sufferer or spreader of disease: again, the immigrant (who has a different skin color).

It should also be noted that Goffman, also in other texts, offered profoundly acute *insights*, often expressed in a few elegant arguments. Take, for example, these lines in which Goffman subtly addresses the inability of people with mental disorders to follow the dictates of "good" communication. Here, he reverses his dramaturgical perspective by showing the difficulty of pretending to be normal. People suffering from addictions are unable to sustain a dialog, because they are making such an effort to observe ritual rules, and not because they are breaching those rules:

> *It is in this narrow space between being out of tune with the encounter and giving it away that drinkers, drug addicts and emotionally distraught people gather, because they are very concerned with hiding their disinterest in the obligations of interaction. (Goffman, 2003, p. 55)*

Goffman assumes that the participants in the interaction afford a sacred value to it. Maintaining the common definition of the situation is a social obligation, but some sick people are unable to do so. Or they may be considered sick precisely because they do not feel its importance.

THE SOCIAL CONSTRUCTION OF HEALTH

My mother is Swedish (but born in Estonia). I was born in Stockholm in 1968, but after a few years, we came to live in Italy, in Rimini, on the Adriatic coast. We lived in my father's family home and my grandparents and great-grandparents also lived below our flat. One day my great-grandfather (Francesco, known as Frazkin) came up to say hello. My mother asked him if he wanted coffee, but my great-grandfather said no. So she did not make him one. The next day, my mother heard from my grandmother that my great-grandfather had complained that "the German had not even offered him a coffee." Although my mother had a good knowledge of the grammar of the

Italian language, she was not so well-versed in the grammar of Italian social relations. Semiologists would say that she was familiar with semantics, but not pragmatics. This is the correct structure of the conversation for the local culture:

> *Mum: Good morning Frazkin, would you like a coffee?*
>
> *Great-grandfather: No, no*
>
> *Mum: Sure?*
>
> *Great-grandfather: Eh no...*
>
> *Mum: I'm making one for myself anyway*
>
> *Great-grandfather: Well, in that case...*
>
> *Mum: Sure, it's no bother!*
>
> *Great-grandfather: Go on then, just a moliga ["a crumb" – a typical local rhetorical figure meaning "a little"]*
>
> *Mum: Oh, come on, a little coffee never did anyone any harm...*

Unfortunately, it didn't play out like that, and my great-grandfather, in a way that would be considered vaguely racist today, lumped my mother in with the Germans (meaning everyone living north of Bozen, and, therefore, cold and insensitive).

I must say my mother was never offended by this. Indeed, just to bring us closer to the question of health, she never even believed in draughts causing neck pain, as all good Italians do.

The purpose of this anecdote is to introduce a basic concept of the social sciences: culture. It is difficult to overestimate the weight of culture in health. Indeed, it is difficult to overestimate the role of culture in every sphere of people's lives. In the social sciences, culture coincides with the set of social representations, beliefs, and norms that shape, influence, and give form to the actions of individuals. Culture regards not only mental aspects but also social practices, ways of doing things, and material objects.

In some cultures, family comes before honesty. In some cultures, punctuality is sacred, while in others, an appointment is seen more as a suggestion than an obligation. In certain cultures, there is a specific dress code for business meetings. Cultures also dictate the timing of various rituals, such as courtship. Culture does not align with the state, although language is probably the most important cultural object in a society.

In the field of health, it is possible to identify numerous socio-cultural representations of illness that have stigmatized the sick person. Given its sexual transmission and its prevalence among the gay community, AIDS had a strong negative connotation in the 1980s, associated with licentiousness, immorality, and deviance. For some religious institutions, AIDS was a punishment for "deviant" sexual behaviors.

Susan Sontag studied the metaphors and cultural meanings associated with cancer and AIDS. The mechanism of stigmatization works like this: a meaning (z) is ascribed to illness (x), so by extension, the meaning (z) is ascribed to (k), who suffers from (x).

When an illness is loaded with meanings, those meanings slowly and gradually take the place of the illness and are realized in practice. This happened regularly for cancer in the 1970s:

> *As long as a particular disease is treated as an evil, invincible predator, not just a disease, most people with cancer will indeed be demoralized by learning what disease they have. The solution is hardly to stop telling cancer patients the truth, but to rectify the conception of the disease, to de-mythicize it. (Sontag, 1978, p. 7)*

In other words:

> *The metaphors and myths, I was convinced, kill (for instance, they make people irrationally fearful of effective measures, such as chemotherapy, and foster credence in thoroughly useless remedies such as diets and psychotherapy). (Sontag, 1989, p. 101)*

The metaphors, in short, follow the famous Thomas Theorem: "If men define situations as real, they are real in their consequences."

Transposed to the field of disease, this theorem could be formulated as follows:

> *I had indeed sadly observed that the metaphorical trappings that deform the experience of being a cancer patient have real consequences: they prevent patients from seeking treatment early enough or making a greater effort to undergo adequate treatment. (Sontag, 1989, p. 101)*

In short, regarding her work *Disease as Metaphor*, Sontag says:

> *I hoped to get them to consider cancer as just a disease: a very serious one, but a disease nonetheless. A phenomenon without "meaning," and not necessarily a death sentence (one of the mystifications is cancer = death). (Sontag, 1978, p. 102)*

Byron Good (1994), a prominent medical anthropologist, has extensively explored how different cultures conceive of illness. His work emphasizes the following key ideas:

- *Cultural variability*: Different societies interpret and respond to illness based on their cultural beliefs, symbols, and practices.
- *Illness as meaning*: In many cultures, illness is not only a biological problem but also a manifestation of social, spiritual, or moral issues. It may be seen as a punishment, a test, or a form of social disorder.
- *Biological versus social conceptions*: Western biomedical models typically understand illness as purely biological, while many other cultures incorporate social and spiritual dimensions into their understanding.
- *Healing practices*: The way illness is conceptualized influences healing practices – whether these involve medication, rituals, or social reintegration.

In summary, Byron Good emphasizes that conceptions of illness are culturally constructed, and understanding these differences is crucial for effective health interventions and cross-cultural medicine. However, although in Western societies disease is regarded as a biological fact, this does not preclude it from having social meanings (as we have seen with AIDS and cancer).

Clearly, cultural aspects also influence behavior and practices not immediately related to health. Consider, for example, the custom of eating the meat of wild animals in China. Or fox hunting in Britain. This can also be applied to countless attitudes toward the environment: from the use of water bottles instead of plastic bottles to the general propensity of the population to vote for "green" parties.

Just as there are several social representations of cancer, beauty, or success – just to mention a few examples – there are also social constructions of environmental problems. As such, it is fundamental to investigate:

> *the process through which environmental claims-makers influence those who hold the reins of power to recognize definitions of environmental problems, to implement them and to accept responsibility for their solution. (Hannigan, 1995, p. 185)*

According to some scholars that adhere to the social construction theory, the "successful" construction of an environmental problem requires six components:

> *the scientific authority for and validation of claims; the existence of "popularisers" (activists, scientists) who can frame and package the "problem" to journalists, political leaders, and other opinion makers; media attention that frames the problem as novel and important (such as the problems of rainforest destruction or ozone depletion); the dramatization of the problem in symbolic or visual terms; visible economic incentives for taking positive action; and the emergence of an institutional sponsor who can ensure legitimacy and continuity of the problem. (Hannigan, 1995, p. 55)*

Mayer (2012) carried out an exhaustive study of the print media's coverage of the relationship between asthma and air pollution, focusing on the way in which the three largest US newspapers depicted a causal link between exposure to air pollution and the occurrence of the disease over a 20-year period. Although the print media's coverage of asthma and its environmental correlates had increased over time, Mayer found that there was little consistency in how the relationship was illustrated; sometimes, air pollution was portrayed as the direct cause of asthma, and sometimes, it was simply represented as a triggering agent. On this basis, Mayer concluded that:

> *This lack of coherence and specificity in the portrayal of asthma as an environmental disease may weaken regulators' ability to act in passing air pollution reform by lowering the public interest and concern. (Mayer, 2012, p. 892)*

The social construction perspective, which is less "ambitious" in proposing a theoretical framework for understanding the relationship between individuals and their environment, is strategically different from critical theory. Rather than offering a comprehensive sociological view of environmental and health problems, the social construction perspective provides a solid methodological basis for empirical investigations. This is both its strength and its weakness.

GREGORY BATESON'S ECOLOGY OF MIND

Gregory Bateson was a singular thinker. Son of the well-known English geneticist William Bateson, he was named Gregory in honor of Mendel, the founder of genetics. Although he graduated in biology, Bateson dedicated his studies to anthropology and psychiatry. He was also profoundly influenced by cybernetics and by systems theory, which he came into contact with while working at the US Office of Strategic Studies during World War II. Many of his theories would later achieve renown thanks to the so called Palo Alto School, which placed them at the basis of systemic psychology. In the field of sociology, his theories have been taken up in the eco-systemic approach. Bateson's own description of his approach is "ecology of the mind" – where the mind can be seen as the equivalent of the ecosystem, while ecology would be the (systemic) mode of analysis. The idea is that man is only a part of a larger whole, composed of organisms, ideas, and relationships. In my view, this perspective anticipated Bruno Latour's *Science, Technology and Society* approach, which argues that society can be seen as a set of interacting human and non-human actors. Today, we humans effectively interact constantly with non-human actors such as algorithms, mobile phone functions, digital platforms (and *vice versa*). With regard to OH, it is useful to introduce four of Bateson's concepts: conscious finalism, complementary/symmetrical relations, communication and metacommunication, and the concept of frame.

With respect to *conscious finalism*, Bateson criticizes the idea, derived from Descartes, of the opposition between subject and object. According to Bateson, Western man has lost sight of *systemic wisdom* and, therefore, regards nature as an other-from-himself that can be controlled and manipulated for his own purposes. Man – the *self* – is a system embedded in other systems and composed, in turn, of other systems. By also conceiving the individual in systemic terms, Bateson denies that "one part can control the whole" and opposes the absolutization of consciousness. It is a logical consequence of the relationship between the whole and the part that a part cannot reproduce the whole system in which it is included, because then the system would be changed and would no longer be the system described previously. According to Bateson, Western man has lost sight of the systemic-holistic nature of the environment. Man intervenes in nature through a finalistic approach and only emphasizes the short span of circuits on which he intervenes in terms of cause-effect. Instead, as we know, an intervention in one part of the system always entails a restructuring, even a minor one, of the whole system, because of the interdependence between the parts the system is composed of. For Bateson,

> *consciousness is organized in terms of purpose. It is a short-cut device to enable you to get quickly at what you want; not to act with maximum wisdom in order to live, but to follow the shortest logical or causal path to get what you next want, which may be dinner; it may be a Beethoven sonata; it may be sex. Above all, it may be money or power. (Bateson, 1972, p. 448)*

Another very important concept in Bateson is the relationship. The scholar distinguishes between *symmetrical* and *complementary* relations.

> *If, in a binary relationship, the behaviors of A and the behaviors of B are considered (by A and by B) to be similar, and A and B are connected to each other in such a way that if A reinforces that behavior, this causes it to be accentuated by B, and vice versa, then the relationship is, with regard to these behaviors, "symmetrical" (an example is competition). If, on the other hand, the behaviors of A and B are dissimilar, but complement each other (such as admiration complementing exhibitionism), and the behaviors are linked in such a way that a reinforcement of A's behavior causes an accentuation of B's corresponding behavior, then the relationship is, with regard to these behaviors, "complementary." (Bateson, 1972, p. 356)*

In everyday life, our relationships are almost always a mix of complementary and symmetrical. Completely symmetrical or completely complementary relationships lead to an "escape," an escalation, which can lead to the collapse of the system (*schismogenesis*, i.e., "progressive differentiation").

Bateson also distinguishes between verbal language and metacommunication. While verbal language has, for the most part, an *informational* function, paralanguage – gestures, tones of voice, interjections, the physical distance between speakers – has a *metacommunicative* function. To put it simply, we could say that verbal language is for talking about things, while metacommunication is for communicating about the relationship we are having. People need signs (e.g., gestures) through which they communicate about (verbal) signs: second-degree, metacommunicative signs. *Metacommunication* performs the function of classifying the messages emitted and received by an organism. Classifying messages means assigning them to the appropriate logical type: messages can refer to events, to previous messages (*metalanguage*), or to the relationship that the actors have established through them (*metacommunication*). The emoticons we use when texting, therefore, have a metacommunicative function.

Another important contribution of Bateson is the concept of frame. Bateson distinguishes between ontology and epistemology. Ontology deals with what the world is like, what things are like, while epistemology investigates how we know the world. If we think of ourselves, of human beings, reality, and knowledge of reality are two sides of the same coin. In everyday life, ontology and epistemology are inextricably intertwined: we think the world is what we see. And what we see, or our experiences, usually confirms the guidelines of our behavior. In the words of Bateson:

> *His [man's] (usually unconscious) beliefs about the world around him will determine the way he sees and acts in it, and this way he feels and acts will determine his beliefs about the nature of the world. (Bateson, 1972, p. 345)*

In short, in human action, ontological premises and epistemological premises are dangerously confused. Knowledge and reality are self-confirming and mutually validating. Experiences lead to the formation of habits and assumptions that will later govern the way we perceive events. We human beings make sense of reality through our cognitive frame:

> *a system of interpretations which we place on the contexts we encounter. (Bateson, 1979, p. 157)*

It will become increasingly easy, in the course of a person's development, to attribute meaning to external events, but it will become increasingly difficult to realize how one gives meaning to the things and social relationships in which one is involved. In other words, by creating the context of his action, man molds it until it is consistent with the desired segmentation, and the context cannot be falsified by the actions that take place within it, since those actions are of an inferior logical type. A simple example: if we have a pessimistic view of life, that is, if our cognitive categories induce us to pre-structure a framework of victim mentality and distrust around our actions, then it is likely that if we play bingo and do not win, we will blame our "congenital" bad luck (and not probability theory).

OH's operational approach can, therefore, only be ecosystemic and based on the realization that one part, namely man, cannot "control the whole..."As Bateson says, the "whole" is made up of interdependent parts. If we destroy the environment, we also suffer, and zoonosis is only one of many possible consequences. This is why Bateson considers it necessary to develop more "systemic wisdom."

HOW CAN SOCIOLOGICAL THEORIES BE USED IN THE OH APPROACH?

Sociological theories on health can be used by the OH approach in different ways. They can undoubtedly have practical applications, guiding research or interventions. But they can also be useful as a set of concepts for a better understanding of the potential of OH. Below are some examples. These examples are not exhaustive in terms of the potential of sociological theories for OH. Depending on specific interests, the theories can certainly also be used for areas of theory, research, and intervention other than those proposed here.

Sociological theories on health inequalities. It is not difficult to see the connections between OH and sociological theories on health inequalities. For example, the most disadvantaged individuals are also those most exposed to the negative consequences of urbanization and the destruction of the natural environment. This can also be seen by reversing the perspective. If we focus on urban expansion and sprawl, especially in Asia and Africa, we can clearly see how the consequences of this "progress" are borne by the most vulnerable populations. Continuing with the examples, another consequence can be found with the concept of syndemics. In general terms, a syndemic is defined as the concomitance of two pathological conditions. Syndemic is not synonymous with co-morbidity, because often one of the two conditions is a risk situation rather than an established disease. For example, the concomitance of an infection and a weak lung. To be more specific, in the case of COVID-19, we know that the effects were much more severe on obese people and people with respiratory problems. Obesity and smoking are more prevalent among people with a low socioeconomic status than better-off people. Other examples can also be cited for the people most at risk of zoonoses (and here, we could also refer to urbanization).

The critical approach. This perspective belongs to a different category from the others. The critical approach is a very broad theory. It can also include sociological theories on health inequalities and the proposal of the political economy of health. It is a broad approach, or in other words, a wide-range theory. As can be seen in the *Unclusions*, the very function of the sociology of health, in relation to OH, may, in part, be a critical perspective.

The social construction of health. The social construction of health theory can be seen above all as a methodology of analysis potentially applicable to all dimensions of OH. Everything we communicate about is, in part, a social construction. Indeed, for some sociologists, it is precisely the way we communicate that constructs our objects. Even scientific objects. There can also be different constructions/representations of the same object, which can also be in contradiction with each other. In the case of OH, we can question how air pollution is portrayed in the media, or how people have different conceptions of antibiotic use. We can also question how there are different conceptions of sustainability, alternative energies, or vaccines. Social stigma is a clear example of how social constructions have real effects on people's lives.

Social stigma theory. An example particularly pertinent to OH is Chagas disease. Chagas disease or American trypanosomiasis is a parasitic disease originating from and endemic in Latin America. It is caused by triatomine bugs that live in the cracks in the walls and roofs of houses made of adobe and straw in rural South America and is spread to humans mainly by vector transmission. Although Chagas disease is a serious infectious disease, it often carries a social stigma, especially in communities where it is endemic. Because it is linked to degraded environments and daily life in close proximity to animals, Chagas disease is a disease linked to poverty, so sufferers feel ashamed. This stigma can manifest itself as discrimination, social exclusion, and reluctance to access medical care. Some scholars have reflected on the practical consequences that can derive from a restrictive viewpoint on the biomedical aspects of Chagas disease:

> *The reproduction of prejudices leads to stick to attitudes of blaming and stigmatisation towards the people affected by Chagas disease themselves, preventing in turn to enquire about the underlying causes that bring together in the problem persistence, whereas the association between rurality and poverty, established by most of the biomedical professionals, reflects the prejudices associated with the non-urban way of life. This viewpoint ignores, and usually disregards, the value of traditions, habits, and practices of certain groups affected by the problematic so that the experts become the only ones trained to provide solutions to improve the affected people's lives. (Sanmartino et al., 2020, p. 66)*

Ecology of mind. Gregory Bateson's perspective consists of a set of concepts that can provide a very clear theoretical scaffold for OH. For example, the concept of the frame, now commonly used in the language of the social sciences but originally proposed by Bateson, can probably help us to think "outside the box," as we say today. And to embrace the OH paradigm, we must do just that: change the cognitive frame we use to view the world, and thus think a little like veterinarians, a little like sociologists, a little like doctors, a little like environmental experts... Bateson's concepts that we have reported here help us to understand the form of animal-environment-people interactions. They allow us to grasp the interdependencies and interactions that take place in the ecosystem (of which we are a part).

REFERENCES

Bateson, G. (1972). *Steps to an ecology of mind*. Chandler. [It. vers.: (1976) Verso un'ecologia della mente, Milano: Adelphi]

Bateson, G. (1979). *Mind and nature: A necessary unity*. Dutton. [It. vers.: (1984). Mente e Natura. Un'unità necessaria. Milano: Adelphi]

Farmer, P. (2005). *Pathologies of power: Health, human rights, and the new war on the poor*. University of California Press.

Goffman, E. (1959). *The presentation of self in everyday life*. Vintage (Penguin).

Goffman, E. (1963). *Stigma: Notes on the management of the spoiled identity*. Touchstone. [It. vers.: (1983). Stigma: Identità negata, Milano: Giuffrè]

Good, B. J. (1994). *Medicine, rationality and experience: An anthropological perspective*. Cambridge University Press. [It. vers.: (2006). Narrare la malattia. Lo sguardo antropologico sul rapporto medico-paziente. Torino: Einaudi]

Hannigan, J. A. (1995). *Environmental sociology: A social constructionist perspective*. Routledge.

Illich, I. (1973). *Limits to medicine – Medical Nemesis: The expropriation of health*. Marion Boyars Publisher Ltd. [It. vers.: (1991). Nemesi medica. L'espropriazione della salute, Milano: Red Edizioni]

Mayer, B. (2012). "Relax and take a deep breath": Print media coverage of asthma and air pollution in the United States. *Social Science & Medicine*, *75*(5), 892–900. https://doi.org/10.1016/j.socscimed.2012.04.024

Mirowski, M. A. et al. (2000). Links between social status and health status. In C. E. Bird, P. Conrad, & A. M. Fremont (Eds.), *Handbook of medical sociology*. Prentice Hall.

Sanmartino, M., Avaria Saavedra, A., & de la Torre Ávila, L. (2020). A social approach to Chagas disease: A first step to improve access to comprehensive care. In M. J. Pinazo Delgado & J. Gascón (Eds.), *Chagas disease*. Springer. https://doi.org/10.1007/978-3-030-44054-1_4

Scambler, G., & Hopkins, A. (1986). Being epileptic: Coming to terms with stigma. *Sociology of Health & Illness*, *8*(1), 26–43. https://doi.org/10.1111/1467-9566.ep11346455

Scavarda, A. (2021). *Pinguini nel deserto. Strategie di resistenza allo stigma da Autismo e Trisomia 21*. Il Mulino.

Sontag, S. (1978). *Illness as metaphor*. Farrar, Straus and Giroux.

Sontag, S. (1989). *AIDS and its metaphors*. Farrar, Straus and Giroux.

5

ONE HEALTH: SOME THEORIES OF JUSTICE

ABSTRACT

This chapter examines the ethical complexity of the One Health (OH) framework by exploring five interconnected forms of justice – environmental, intergenerational, interspecies, social and epistemic – and assessing how they can be integrated into a cohesive ethical orientation. It begins by discussing environmental justice (EJ), showing how unequal exposure to environmental risks disproportionately harms marginalized communities and ecosystems, and how concepts such as post-growth, the New Ecological Paradigm (NEP) and social-ecological systems can inform OH's holistic perspective. The chapter then addresses intergenerational justice, linking sustainability, future generations' rights and the responsibility to preserve environmental options, quality and access. Drawing on thinkers such as Edith Brown Weiss, it highlights how intergenerational equity requires both institutional reforms and anticipatory capacities, including futures literacy and foresight methodologies. The third dimension, interspecies justice, expands moral consideration to non-human animals, emphasizing their intrinsic value, the harms of intensive farming and the need for ethically and ecologically responsible food systems aligned with OH principles. The chapter then turns to social justice and intersectionality, explaining how overlapping inequalities create complex causal chains that affect health outcomes. It also introduces the concept of epistemic injustice – testimonial and hermeneutical – showing how marginalized knowledge systems, including indigenous ecological knowledge, are often undervalued within health and environmental governance. The chapter concludes by exploring whether OH can be understood as a form of "extended intersectionality," capable of integrating environmental, temporal, species-based and social dimensions of justice into a unified, relational, and dynamic framework for promoting truly holistic health.

Keywords: Social justice; environmental justice; intergenerational justice; inter-species justice; ethics and One Health; intersectionality

INTRODUCTION

In this chapter, we present different types of justice related to OH. The aim is to demonstrate the complexity of the ethical dimensions involved in OH. At the same time, we provide some guidance on how to place and integrate these different orientations within the multiple dimensions of OH.

Starting with EJ, we analyze how social inequalities influence the distribution of environmental risks and how this translates into health inequalities. We then examine the concept of intergenerational justice, which recalls the responsibility to ensure that the actions we take today do not impact upon the well-being of future generations, in line with the principles of sustainability. We then delve into the concept of intergenerational justice, which recalls the responsibility to ensure that present actions do not compromise the well-being of future generations, in line with the principles of sustainability. We move on to examine inter-species justice, which extends ethical consideration to non-human animals, recognizing their intrinsic value and the need for a more respectful approach to them. After that, we describe the concept of epistemic injustice which deals with the lack of recognition of marginalized social groups knowledge. Finally, we explore social justice and intersectionality, highlighting how inequalities overlap, creating complex causal chains that differentially affect health. We, therefore, seek to understand whether the OH approach can be conceived as a form of "extended intersectionality," able to integrate the different dimensions of justice in a holistic and dynamic vision that is not only related to the human dimension but also extendable to the animal kingdom and the wider ecosystem.

ENVIRONMENTAL JUSTICE

We live on a planet that is becoming increasingly urbanized. By 2050, two-thirds of the population is projected to live in urban areas. It is said that:

> *cities are social-ecological systems characterized by high human density and infrastructure to support human communities. (Murray et al., 2022, p. 403)*

Since "infrastructures" refers to roads, buildings, vehicles, and commercial activities, perhaps cities can be seen primarily as "social-*ego*logical systems" rather than "social-ecological systems" (also because the ecological aspect is an increasingly marginal one). While the pun might make you groan, it's a fact that ever-increasing traffic, air pollution, deforestation, and, thus, urban heat are causes of disease and problems for people, animals, and ecosystems. Above all, these processes put the most vulnerable individuals and marginalized communities at risk. Put simply, environmental risks hit the poor hardest. For example, with regard to urban heat:

> *Lower-income neighborhoods often have less access to green spaces and parks, reduced canopy cover, and lower vegetation overall, thus limiting access to natural cooling strategies and increasing heat vulnerability for some urban residents. (Murray et al., 2022, p. 412)*

It is, therefore, quite logical to say that:

> *the environmental crisis is also a social justice issue, with the most vulnerable populations bearing the brunt of its effects. (Islam, 2024, p. 3)*

To introduce the concept of EJ, it is useful to start with two other ethical and political approaches to the relationship between man and the environment: the Post-Growth Society and the NEP.[1]

The Post-Growth Society paradigm suggests that perpetual economic growth is not only unsustainable but also harmful to the environment and society. The Post-Growth Society paradigm is based on seven principles:

1. Quality of life over quantity of growth (in a post-growth society, the well-being of communities, the natural environment, and public health would take precedence over GDP growth);

2. Rejection of "Growth Mania" (the pursuit of continuous economic growth is an illusion that exacerbates environmental degradation and social inequality);

3. Reshaping corporate power (corporate goals should align with social and environmental priorities);

4. Degrowth as a pathway (shifting societal values from consumerism to sustainability, focusing on sufficiency rather than excess);

5. Localization of economies (promoting localized economies that reduce dependency on global trade and prioritize local production, consumption, and governance);

6. Redistribution of wealth and resources (implementing policies such as progressive taxation, universal basic income, and equitable access to housing);

7. Sustainable use of resources (encouraging resource-efficient technologies and cultural shifts toward reducing consumption to meet environmental and social goals sustainably).

The NEP challenges the traditional human-centered or anthropocentric worldview. Like OH, it argues for a more eco-centric perspective, one that recognizes the interconnectedness of humans with the natural world. The NEP is also rooted in seven key principles:

1. Human dependence on nature (humans depend on the finite biophysical environment for survival, contrary to the widely held belief that technology can fully compensate for ecological degradation);

2. Interconnectedness of species (this recognition urges the protection of biodiversity and the acknowledgment that other species have the right to exist and thrive alongside humans);

3. Limits to growth (the environment imposes constraints on human activity, and humanity cannot bypass the laws of ecology);

4. Ethical obligations to non-human entities (the NEP asserts that plants, animals, and ecosystems possess intrinsic rights to exist independently of human needs or desires);

5. Rejection of technological fixes (the NEP advocates for systemic changes in consumption patterns, lifestyle choices, and governance, to address root causes rather than temporary technological band-aids);

6. Ecological justice (the NEP addresses inequalities between nations, communities, and species, to achieve a balanced and just coexistence within Earth's ecological limits);

7. Sustainable living (the NEP calls for a transition toward sustainable living, emphasizing the need for long-term ecological balance over short-term exploitation of resources).

The EJ paradigm examines how marginalized communities disproportionately bear the burden of environmental degradation, due to unequal laws, regulations, and policies. EJ seeks equitable treatment for all people, regardless of race, ethnicity, income, or geography, in the development, implementation, and enforcement of environmental policies. Below are the eight key principles of the EJ Paradigm.

1. Fair treatment (this principle challenges existing systems of environmental inequality, which often expose marginalized communities to greater risks of pollution and climate-related disasters);
2. Meaningful participation (EJ emphasizes the importance of meaningful participation, ensuring that marginalized and affected communities have a say in the decision-making processes that impact their lives);
3. Non-discrimination (EJ mandates non-discriminatory environmental policies that do not disproportionately harm vulnerable populations);
4. Recognition of rights (The paradigm advocates recognizing the inherent rights of individuals, communities, and ecosystems to a clean and healthy environment. This includes protecting indigenous rights to land);
5. Intergenerational equity (EJ encompasses the principle of intergenerational equity, ensuring that present actions do not compromise the ability of future generations to meet their needs);
6. Community empowerment (EJ stresses the importance of empowering affected communities through education and access to information and resources to advocate for their rights, also supporting grassroots movements);
7. Accountability and transparency (Governments, corporations, and international organizations must be held responsible for environmental harm and provide clear, accessible information to communities);
8. Global solidarity (EJ recognizes the interconnectedness of global struggles, advocating for solidarity among nations and communities to address shared environmental challenges. This includes acknowledging the disproportionate impacts of environmental degradation on the Global South).

This valuable, analytical conceptual reconstruction by Islam (2024), which I have summarized here, provides many insights into the links between health, environment, and justice. In the case of OH, however, it is appropriate to move away slightly from the theoretical reconstruction of the three concepts and to embrace a broader definition of EJ. The OH idea of justice requires the "importation" of many, if not all, of the principles underpinning the NEP, emphasizing the interconnectedness and interdependence that bind individuals, animals, and habitats. Moreover, at least in connection with OH, the other two concepts contain some weaknesses. The Post-Growth Society model has been criticized because, in some cases, it has been possible to demonstrate that nations can achieve growth while reducing or stabilizing emissions (economic decoupling). As far as the NEP is concerned, while its success in downplaying anthropocentrism and its apt emphasis on the interconnectedness of species should be acknowledged,

> *by focusing primarily on humanity's relationship with the environment, NEP risks insufficiently addressing the social, economic, and political disparities that exacerbate climate vulnerability, particularly for marginalized communities. (Islam, 2024, p. 9)*

Moreover, challenging though it is, especially for those accustomed to sociological observation, a dis-location is necessary to shift our attention toward the relationships between the three dimensions OH is composed of and thus see environmental damage as an injustice in itself rather than just an injustice because the effects of environmental damage fall on the most vulnerable social groups. This fundamental dimension is the focus of social justice. However, the OH vision, alongside social justice, also requires us to look further, focusing on the ecosystem as a whole. On relationships and not just on things. It is no coincidence that anthropology speaks of "relational ontology," that is, the idea that nothing exists apart from relationships. In other words, things and people are constituted by the relationships between them and do not exist *a priori* (Escobar, 2016).

The concept of socio-ecological system (SES) proposed by Elinor Ostrom is particularly suitable for connecting OH and EJ (Ostrom, 2005, 2009). There is a solid link between Elinor Ostrom's SES concept and the OH approach: both are based on a holistic and integrated perspective to address complex challenges involving health, the environment, and human communities. In essence, Ostrom's framework offers a method for analyzing the systems that OH seeks to preserve. More specifically, the SES can be defined as a complex and interconnected system in which humans and nature are inextricably linked, where local communities can self-manage common resources in a sustainable manner through well-defined rules and institutions adapted to the specific context. This is an integrative and multidisciplinary approach to understanding complex interactions within different systems and scales around the governance of natural resources. Ostrom's work highlights the importance of collaborative governance and the participation of local communities in the management of shared resources. Similarly, OH promotes collaboration between different sectors (health policy, environmental policy, agricultural policy, the non-profit sector) and the engagement of local communities to address environmental and health challenges effectively. The idea is that complex problems can only be tackled with multi-sectoral and multi-dimensional approaches, and not by means based on today's fashionable ideals of "technological solutionism."

In summary:

- Ostrom's approach can be used to analyze the management of zoonotic diseases, considering the interactions between wild animals, livestock, human communities and health systems.
- Ostrom's framework can help design sustainable natural resource management strategies that take into account impacts on human and animal health.
- Ostrom's governance principles can guide the creation of OH governance systems that promote collaboration and participation between different sectors and levels of government.

In summary, Ostrom's social–ecological system framework offers a useful lens through which to analyze and improve the efficacy of OH initiatives, providing an EJ approach to understanding complexity, promoting collaborative governance, and ensuring the sustainability of solutions. Ostrom's framework thus highlights how human communities are embedded within complex ecological systems and how their actions influence the health and sustainability of those systems. Likewise, OH emphasizes that human health is inextricably linked to the health of animals and the health of the ecosystems we live in. Elinor Ostrom won the Nobel Prize for Economics in 2009.

INTERGENERATIONAL JUSTICE

Talking about intergenerational justice necessarily requires a reference to the principle of sustainability. The document entitled *United Nations System Common Principles on Future Generations* states that:

> *Fairness between generations is embedded in the concept of sustainable development: the needs of present generations must not be met at the expense of generations to come. (United Nations System – Chief Executives Board for Coordination, 2023)*

The importance of sustainability has been reinvigorated globally by the United Nations' 2030 Agenda for Sustainable Development (2030 Agenda) and its 17 Sustainable Development Goals. When striving toward sustainable development, it is essential that intergenerational equity, a key pillar of sustainable development, is not overlooked.

To be analytical, we should distinguish between intergenerational equity, intergenerational justice, and intergenerational solidarity. Intergenerational equity is the goal; intergenerational justice is the means by which intergenerational equity is ensured, while intergenerational solidarity is the principle that should guide concrete actions and that should produce social cohesion between different generations. When we speak of intergenerational justice, we are referring to future generations. It is also necessary to mention the classic distinction between *inter*generational justice and *intra*generational justice. The distinction is based on two different types of duty.

> *First, "an intergenerational duty owed by each generation to its successors"; and second, "an intragenerational duty owed to members of the same generation." (Brown Weiss, 1984, p. 499)*

However, it should be emphasized that several generations coexist at any given time (elderly people, adults, young people, children: all different generations).

As mentioned, sustainability is closely linked to intergenerational justice. And sustainability is the point where intergenerational justice meets a nature-friendly and ecology-friendly approach. To return to the *United Nations System Common Principles on Future Generations*:

> *The recognition of human rights of future generations, and corresponding duties, will also be affected by whether an anthropocentric and/or eco-centric approach is applied to policymaking. The relationship that humanity has with the natural world will necessarily have implications for the rights and duties framework. Beyond the human right to a clean, healthy and sustainable environment, the growing recognition of rights of*

> *nature at national or subnational levels, as well as increasingly valuing other non-formal knowledge systems, for instance from Indigenous Peoples, local or traditional communities, can support keeping future generations at the heart of the rights and duties framework. (United Nations System – Chief Executives Board for Coordination, 2023, p. 8)*

The document goes on to highlight the importance of "future literacy," that is, the ability to make choices taking into account possible changes in scenarios, and "foresight," that is, the competence to use appropriate methodologies to imagine the future and thus be able to plan appropriate policies. Whereas future literacy refers to individuals, forecasting refers to institutions. Future studies play an important role in the OH approach. As we can see in Chapter 3, future studies methodologies can help OH practitioners to anticipate emerging health threats arising from changes in demographics, climate, land use, technology, and social behavior. For example, scenario planning can help explore different potential pathways for the emergence and spread of zoonotic diseases under various climate change scenarios.

A scholar of particular relevance to intergenerational justice is Edith Brown Weiss. Underlying her theory of intergenerational equity is the principle of the environment as the "common heritage" of humanity. This common heritage is passed on from one generation to the next. Each generation has an obligation to preserve it for future generations. Brown Weiss proposes an extended notion of environment, encompassing natural resources, ecosystems, biodiversity, and even cultural heritage. Her generational equity perspective (1989) is developed according to three principles:

- *Conservation of options*: Each generation should leave future generations a range of environmental options no less broad than the one they inherited. This means that we should avoid actions that irreversibly impact resources or biodiversity;
- *Conservation of quality*: Each generation should leave future generations an environment of at least the same quality as the one they inherited. This means that we should strive to reduce pollution, protect ecosystems, and manage natural resources sustainably;
- *Conservation of access*: Each generation should guarantee future generations fair access to environmental resources. This means that we should avoid concentrating wealth and power in the hands of a few, to the detriment of future generations.

In a 2008 article, Brown Weiss proposes criteria that should make the three principles less abstract. Those criteria are balance, flexibility, cultural acceptability, and clarity:

> *One criterion is to balance the needs of future generations with those of the present, neither licensing the present generation to consume without attention to the interests of future generations or requiring it to sacrifice unreasonably to meet indeterminate future needs. Since we cannot predict the values of future generations, we also have to provide them with the options and quality to satisfy their own values and needs. In addition, the principles need to be generally acceptable to the many different cultures in the world, and finally, they have to be reasonably clear so that they can be implemented and applied. (Brown Weiss, 2008, pp. 616–617)*

One of the most original aspects of Brown Weiss' thought is the role she assigns to international law. Her theory criticizes the traditional approach to international law, which focuses mainly on relations between states and does not take into account the interests of future generations. As early as 1989, Weiss argued that international law must evolve to incorporate the principles of intergenerational equity. This requires the creation of rules and institutions that promote the sustainable management of natural resources and protect the rights of future generations. The OH approach, with its emphasis on interdependence and sustainability, could provide the scientific evidence base on which to develop international conventions to guarantee the rights of future generations.

INTERSPECIES JUSTICE

Since prehistoric times, there has been intense interaction between humans, or rather, human animals, and non-human animals. Animals were bred and eaten, and clothes were made from their skins. Furthermore, there was a strong spiritual bond with animals, testified to by prehistoric rock art. At a certain point, however, things changed...

> *Starting about 10,000 years ago, the human relationship with wild animals was transformed. Domestication changed this relationship into one of dominance and control as humans took on the role of master. Animals – no longer wild – became classified as property,*

> *and were considered items to be owned and exchanged. Today, domesticated animals can be bred, controlled, abused, or killed as the owner desires. (De Mello, 2012, pp. 67–68)*

From a neo-Marxist perspective (Nibert, 2013), it is also plausible to attribute

> *the rise in gender inequality to the development of organized hunting and animal domestication, which lead to unequal divisions of labour, the devaluation of women's labour and male control of surplus wealth. This surplus wealth (widely measured by one's ownership of animals) necessitated the creation of a "warrior class" and "priestly class" to defend and manage this wealth. (Koop-Montero, 2023, p. 1146)*

As we have already seen in this chapter, the New Ecology Paradigm developed in the 1970s. The NEP highlights humanity's reciprocal relationship with nature and the biological limits of the environment, whereas until then, in the social sciences, the Human Exceptionalism Paradigm (HEP) approach had been dominant. This approach was based on the idea that the prominence of human culture, given its dynamism, would help humans overcome natural limits of the environment. Clearly, the HEP remains by far the dominant paradigm today, yet the NEP has contributed to the emergence of a new sensitivity to the environment. It should be noted that this "new ecology" also recognizes animal rights, and not only the environmental dimension in the strictest sense.

Worth mentioning at this point is the contribution of the Australian philosopher Peter Singer, who in 1975 published the volume *Animal Liberation*. Singer is known for popularizing the concept of "speciesism," which he defines as a prejudice or bias in favor of one's own species (humans) over others. He argues that this bias is morally wrong, in a similar way to sexism and racism, because it unfairly privileges the interests of one group (humans) over another (non-human animals). His work has been foundational to the modern animal rights movement and to the development of the notion of interspecies justice.

Singer's argument against speciesism centers on the principle of equal consideration of interests. He argues that if we are concerned with the suffering of humans, we should also be concerned with the suffering of other beings capable of experiencing pain and pleasure, regardless of their species. Singer contends that the capacity for suffering – not species membership – is the relevant characteristic for determining moral consideration. Therefore, if a being can suffer, its interests should be given equal weight to similar interests of any other being. This ability to suffer and to enjoy life gives them intrinsic value and thus the right not to be mistreated or exploited:

> *Can they suffer? Can they enjoy life? If so, they have interests that we should take into account, and we should give those interests equal weight with the interests of all other beings with similar interests. We should not discount their interests in not suffering because they cannot talk or because they are incapable of reasoning; and we should not discount their interests in enjoying life, in having things that are fulfilling and rewarding for them, either. The principle of equal consideration of interests should apply to both humans and animals. That's the sense in which I want to elevate animals to the moral status of humans. (Singer, 2009, p. 576)*

Unlike the anthropocentric view, which sees animals as resources or tools at the service of humans, interspecies justice recognizes that animals have value in themselves, regardless of their usefulness to humans. Interspecies justice implies both negative obligations (not to cause harm, not to exploit) and positive obligations (to protect, to assist). While interspecies justice derives from EJ (because it deals with the specific aspect of the ecosystem that is animals), in other respects, it intersects with dimensions of restorative justice. In addition to preventing future damage, inter-species justice can also require reparation for damage that has been caused to animals in the past. This could involve the rehabilitation of degraded habitats, the creation of sanctuaries for animals rescued from farms or laboratories, or the recognition and redress of historical injustices to animals.

In a perspective of inter-species justice, intensive livestock farms should be closed. In addition to the killing of animals, intensive livestock farming produces very worrying externalities and is, therefore, also deplorable from a OH perspective. Intensive livestock farming poses a real threat to all three pillars of OH. This mode of food production creates an environment favorable to the emergence and spread of zoonotic diseases, due to the high density of animals, the poor hygiene, and the stress to which the animals are subjected, favoring the mutation and transmission of dangerous viruses and bacteria. At the same time, the massive and often prophylactic use of antibiotics in intensive livestock breeding fuels antibiotic resistance, making treatment for infections in humans more difficult and expensive. The negative impacts are not limited to health and extend to the environment: intensive livestock farming makes a significant contribution to air, water, and soil pollution, releasing greenhouse gases that accelerate climate change, as well as contaminating water resources. Although they have increased food production, these systems also raise serious food safety concerns, due to potential drug residues and the risk of spreading diseases.

The sustainability dimension also occupies a central role in the case of inter-species justice. Although they focus on different aspects, sustainability and inter-species justice are closely linked by a common thread: concern for long-term well-being and equity (a conceptual core that, of course, also resonates deeply with the principles of OH). If truly practiced, sustainability – by reducing pollution, protecting resources and mitigating climate change – creates the conditions for a future in which the needs of the generations to come can also be met. For its part, inter-species justice complements this vision by extending ethical consideration also to non-human animals, recognizing their intrinsic value and the need for equitable consideration of their interests. This approach reflects OH's holistic vision, which considers the health of humans, animals, and ecosystems to be interconnected.

In this perspective, inter-species justice reinforces the objectives of both the sustainability principle and OH, rendering them more complete. Meeting the challenges of One Health, such as the emergence of zoonotic diseases or antibiotic resistance, inevitably requires us to reconsider our relationship with animals and to promote farming practices that respect their well-being. A future-oriented approach cannot only ensure the prosperity of human generations, and must also protect the health and well-being of all sentient species, recognizing our interdependence with the natural world (as well as future generations). In practice, this means promoting a development model that is not only ecologically sustainable, but also ethically fair toward animals and consistent with the principles of One Health, moving toward food systems that respect animal welfare, and ensuring that the interests of animals are considered in every decision regarding them, in order to guarantee a single health shared by all living beings.

SOCIAL JUSTICE AND INTERSECTIONALITY

We have already implicitly dealt with social justice in the perspective of health. For the most part, social justice in the area of health coincides with the recognition of the weight of social inequality in making people's lives difficult, burdensome, and painful. Consequently, a social justice approach not only identifies the social and economic factors that cause suffering and illness but also aims to implement broad health policies aimed at countering the very origins of health inequalities. So it's a question of intervening on the social determinants of health; of showing its weight and coming up with actions to reduce its negative influence. Given the heterogeneity of the social determinants of health, interventions must necessarily be of different types and conducted by different actors: they must be transdisciplinary and multi-sectoral actions.

In the last decade, social justice has increasingly been conceived in connection with intersectionality theory. Intersectionality theory is not only a tool for investigating health inequalities. It is also a real way of rethinking social inequality, and indeed the entire organization of society, and, therefore, contains an ethical aspect and a strong tension toward social justice. We can present this theory starting from the Bible.

There is a verse in the Gospel of Matthew (13:12) that is especially familiar to sociologists:

> *For whoever has, to him more will be given, and he will have abundance; but whoever does not have, even what he has will be taken away from him.*

This "Matthew effect" was coined by Robert K. Merton. Merton (1968) showed how scientists who had achieved fame at a young age could, as their careers continued, "live off" that fame, so to speak, with their theories abundantly and continually cited in ever-widening circles. In addition, they have an easier time getting published because of their reputation, and not always because of the quality of their writings, whereas lesser-known scholars have to work much harder in proportion. This elegant concept has been applied in numerous fields. For example, studies in the sociology of education have shown that students who master reading and text comprehension from an early age quickly amplify their skills, while those who are still struggling in the third or fourth year of elementary school struggle to attain these two skills suffer throughout their lives. The fact that most of those children with poorer language skills tend to be from socially disadvantaged classes brings us back to the question of inequalities.

The basic assumption of intersectionality theory is that the social factors that produce inequality overlap and form complex, interdependent causal chains. Consequently, it is fallacious to concentrate on and propose interventions focused on single dimensions only. Inequalities accumulate and self-amplify. Collins defines the theory of intersectionality as

> *the critical insight that race, class, gender, sexuality, ethnicity, nation, ability, and age operate not as unitary, mutually exclusive entities, but rather as reciprocally constructing phenomena. (Collins, 2015, p. 1)*

In the field of health policy, it may prove fallacious to target one source of inequality without taking into account the other "sections" a person is composed of. People are made up of multiple "sections" – biological, social, cultural – and each of these traits is connected to the social world in specific ways that are also derived from its other traits. For example, an individual can carry a trait that is stigmatized in many contexts, such as being gay, but have a high level of education and a high income. Sexual identity can have different effects on health, depending on skin color and income, type of employment, and income. In short, the same person is placed in different social positions and is made up of interconnected traits that condition his or her chances of a (healthy) life. When two or more "weak" sections overlap, the negative effects are amplified.

Consistently, an intersectional approach in health policy is not directed toward changing individual risk factors, but toward the root causes of health inequalities, the so called distal factors. However, unlike Marxist theories of inequality, the intersectional approach does not absolutize socio-economic status. On the contrary, it integrates it with other sections of a person's identity and shows their complex interdependencies.

Empirical research based on the concept of intersectionality has mostly been carried out in the field of gender studies and the sociology of ethnicity and has mostly been conducted using qualitative instruments. In recent years, however, there has been an enormous increase in quantitative research, which uses sophisticated statistical tools to estimate the direct or indirect impact of various biological and social factors on people's health, their interdependencies, and their amplifying or reducing effects. The intersectional approach is also used by mathematicians and computer scientists, who study how to reduce the social discrimination that, in some cases, is perpetrated by algorithms.

EPISTEMIC INJUSTICE

The concept of epistemic injustice was popularized by the philosopher Miranda Fricker (2007). It mainly regards the failure to recognize and the systematic underestimation of the opinions and knowledge of disadvantaged social groups. Fricker defines epistemic injustice as

> *a wrong done to someone specifically in their capacity as a knower. (Fricker, 2007, p. 1)*

This definition becomes clearer if we refer to the two types of epistemic injustice proposed by Fricker: testimonial injustice and hermeneutical injustice.

Testimonial injustice occurs when a person's words are given less credibility than they deserve because of a prejudice on the part of the listener. The wrong is typically perpetrated by someone (e.g., a man) belonging to a group that traditionally has more socio-economic power than the group the victim belongs to. As an example, Fricker refers to a scene from the film *The Talented Mr. Ripley in which* Marge has reason to suspect that Ripley killed her boyfriend, Dickie. However, when Marge tries to explain her view of events and her suspicions regarding Ripley, her missing boyfriend's father silences her with the words:

> *Marge, there's female intuition, and then there are facts. (Fricker, 2007, p. 9)*

The injustice in question is epistemic, because it is a prejudice relating to the ability of certain categories of people, such as women, immigrants, or even disabled people, to reason, acquire knowledge and transmit it. Another example offered by Fricker regards a woman who works in a large company, and whose suggestions are always dismissed. So when she wants a certain procedure she has in mind to be implemented, she passes a note with her suggestion to a male colleague, so that he can present it as his own. This significantly increases the chances of the suggestion being effectively acted upon.

Hermeneutical injustice, on the other hand, regards the inability of certain socially vulnerable people to understand things that affect them. This inability is not, however, the result of a cognitive deficit; it is caused by a lack of social concepts and categories that serve to interpret a specific situation of exploitation. More specifically, hermeneutical injustice occurs when

> *a gap in collective interpretive resources puts someone at an unfair disadvantage when it comes to making sense of their social experiences. (Fricker, 2007, p. 9)*

The clearest example provided by Fricker is based on what happened to Carmita Wood, an employee in the Department of Nuclear Physics at Cornell University in the 1970s. Wood had become the target of sexual interest on the part of her boss, Professor Boyce McDaniel. Wood's boss behaved in a sexually aggressive manner:

> *the eminent man would jiggle his crotch when he stood near her desk and looked at his mail. (Fricker, 2007, p. 150)*

In addition, McDaniel found opportunities to deliberately rub against her breasts and attempt to kiss her against her will. As a result of the repeated harassment, Carmita Wood developed a series of psychosomatic disorders and requested a transfer. This request was rejected, and in the end, she resigned. When applying for unemployment benefit, Wood felt at a loss when describing the reasons for her resignation, ultimately citing "personal reasons." She was denied unemployment benefit.

Reading this story today, it seems aberrant. It is clear that Carmita Wood was sexually harassed and subjected to abuse. However, in those years, the term "sexual harassment" did not even exist and, consequently, neither did the crime. There were, therefore, no concepts to label, name, and give meaning to McDaniel's criminal behavior. It was not until years later that, as a result of new sensibilities toward women, words and concepts emerged that aided recognition of these situations of sexual violence. These provided a lexicon for naming certain behaviors and thus creating socially communicable categories. The concept of hermeneutical injustice recalls 1984, except that in Orwell's work, the temporal sequence is reversed: words are destroyed to prevent people from thinking about the concepts they express:

> *Don't you see that the whole aim of Newspeak is to narrow the range of thought? In the end we shall make thoughtcrime literally impossible, because there will be no words in which to express it. (...) Every year fewer and fewer words, and the range of consciousness a little smaller. (Orwell, 1983, p. 46)*[2]

In addition to being abused by her boss and refused unemployment benefit, Carmita Wood suffered what we now call "gaslighting." Gaslighting is a form of psychological manipulation in which a person or group secretly sows seeds of doubt in a targeted individual or group, making them question their own memory, perception, or sanity. The manipulator's goal is to erode the victim's sense of reality and self-trust, leading them to become dependent on the manipulator for their sense of what is real. In the case we have just discussed, however, there is no manipulator in the flesh. There is an unjust, conservative, and patriarchal social conscience that legitimizes a certain power structure.

Going back to the general definition of epistemic injustice, we could say that in the case of testimonial injustice, the knower is not recognized as having the capacity to understand and know things about the world; in the case of epistemic injustice, they are not (even) recognized as having the capacity to understand themselves. Carmita Wood's case probably also includes some elements of testimonial injustice.

More generally, as Fricker explains, many epistemic injustices are *systematic* in nature, in the sense that they are connected to various elements in the social system in such a way that the scope of the injustice is amplified:

> *Systematic testimonial injustices, then, are produced not by prejudice simpliciter, but specifically by those prejudices that "track" the subject through different dimensions of social activity – economic, educational, professional, sexual, legal, political, religious, and so on. Being subject to a tracker prejudice renders one susceptible not only to testimonial injustice but to a gamut of different injustices. (Fricker, 2007, p. 27)*

Fricker entitled her book *Epistemic Injustice*, not *Epistemic Justice*. By making this choice, Miranda Fricker's intention is to emphasize the fact that cases of epistemic injustice are the norm and not the exception. Epistemic injustices are so widespread and frequent that they go unnoticed. Only through careful analysis of social practices and discourse can we deconstruct the multiple dynamics of power and discrimination that are perpetrated daily and almost automatically against the most vulnerable social groups.

The distance between One Health and epistemic injustice is shorter than it might seem.

In many cultures and local communities, particularly indigenous ones, there is established knowledge regarding the management of nature, ecosystems, and relationships with non-human animals. Epistemic injustice occurs when this knowledge is ignored, devalued, or considered less valid than Western scientific knowledge. This results in the risk of losing a wealth of valuable knowledge that could contribute to more sustainable and resilient solutions in the field of environmental health.

In the context of an intervention to promote health, ignoring indigenous knowledge can be seen both as a testimonial injustice (I accept the positions of scientists as true, and not those of the populations living in the area) and as a hermeneutical injustice (I accept only biomedical theories as true, and not the secular beliefs of indigenous peoples). Awareness of the risk of epistemic injustice, also in the context of One Health, highlights the importance of promoting inclusive and participatory processes. Creating One Health policies that recognize the knowledge and testimonies of all communities helps overcome epistemic inequalities, promoting more equitable, sustainable, and shared interventions.

ONE HEALTH: A BROADER VIEW OF INTERSECTIONALITY?

The intersectional approach emphasizes the interdependence and relationships between different social dimensions:

> *Race, class, gender, sexuality, age, ability, nation, ethnicity, and similar categories of analysis are best understood in relational terms rather than in isolation from one another. (Collins, 2015, p. 14)*

The relational nature of the intersectional approach, therefore, requires that social reality be considered a dynamic social process:

> *Because social formations of complex social inequalities are historically contingent and cross-culturally specific, unequal material realities and social experiences vary across time and space. (Collins, 2015, p. 14)*

First, we can emphasize how, despite their different levels of abstraction, both approaches – OH and intersectionality theory – pay special attention to the temporal dimension. Both are interested in change and the different forms that specific "entanglements" can take. This focus is explained by addressing perhaps the most characteristic principle of both epistemologies: interdependence. To analyze and break down the interdependence between different elements and dimensions, it is necessary to break down reality in terms of causal relationships, and to foreground the etiological links, it is necessary to consider temporality, because we know that one cause can produce different effects, just as one effect can be the product of different causes. And we also know that an effect can be produced with a gradualness proportional to the cause or when the cause exceeds a certain threshold (the threshold effect). Moreover, some effects remain latent for a long time, that is, they are there, but do not manifest themselves until after a certain time. So to disarticulate interdependence, we must necessarily refer to causality and (thus) temporality.

Second, both approaches share a holistic view. In the case of OH, this holistic view is one of its fundamental characteristics; in the case of intersectionality, holism is more a consequence of intersectionality's critique of conceptions that look at inequalities by foregrounding a single factor (be it economic, demographic, sexual identity, physical or cognitive abilities…). Clearly, there could be no interdependence without holism and vice versa.

Third, both approaches give importance to marginalized perspectives. One Health criticizes anthropocentric epistemologies, to show the importance of the environment and non-human animals; intersectionality, also thanks to the postcolonial perspective, criticizes ethnocentrism and the absolutization of the Eurocentric perspective and focuses on how various social identities and inequalities intertwine to influence people's living conditions and health.

Speculating a little, we could perhaps conceive of the OH approach as a sort of "extended intersectionality." Indeed, the epistemological peculiarity of

OH is that it avoids anthropomorphism and any precedence within the three dimensions, just as intersectionality, in the context of health inequalities, does not absolutize socio-economic status. This requires significant cognitive effort because, in both cases, it necessitates stepping out of a way of seeing things that has long been taken for granted. In the case of OH, several factors must be identified and weighed, without absolutizing the human, animal, or environmental aspects. Reality thus ultimately coincides with a fabric of dynamic relationships in which all the actors (human, animal, environmental) are interconnected through networks that form and dissolve over time. To take up a concept popularized by Latour, these temporary networks are “assemblages” between heterogeneous elements (Latour, 2005). It is, therefore, important to see the contribution of intersectionality for OH not as a fertilization of OH with sociological concepts, but as an analogy with a holistic and dynamic cognitive perspective that does not absolutize one dimension to the detriment of others. Maintaining this cognitive epistemology makes it possible to hold together the different types of justice described here (environmental justice, intergenerational justice, interspecies justice, social, and intersectional justice) without absolutizing one over the others, except for analyses linked to specific contexts and circumstances.

NOTES

1. A summary of the clear, exhaustive article by Islam (2024, pp. 8–11).
2. The quote is taken from the edition published in 1983 by The New American Library on p. 46.

REFERENCES

Collins, P. H. (2015). Intersectionality’s definitional dilemmas. *Annual Review of Sociology*, *41*, 1–20. https://doi.org/10.1146/annurev-soc-073014-112142

De Mello, M. (2012). *Animals and society: An introduction to human-animal studies*. Columbia University Press.

Escobar, A. (2016). Thinking-feeling with the Earth: Territorial struggles and the ontological dimension of the epistemologies of the South. *Aibr-revista De Antropologia Iberoamericana*, *11*(1), 11–32. https://doi.org/10.11156/AIBR.110102E

Fricker, M. (2007). *Epistemic injustice power & the ethics of knowing*. Oxford University Press.

Islam, M. S. (2024). Rethinking climate justice: Insights from environmental sociology. *Climate*, *12*(12), 1–19. https://doi.org/10.3390/cli12120203

Koop-Montero, Y. (2023). Including animals in sociology. *Current Sociology*, *71*(6), 1141–1158. https://doi.org/10.1177/00113921211065492

Latour, B. (2005). *Reassembling the social: An introduction to actor-network-theory*. Oxford UP.

Merton, R. K. (1968). The Matthew effect in science: The reward and communication systems of science are considered. *Science*, *159*(3810), 56–63. https://doi.org/10.1126/science.159.3810.56

Murray, M. H., Buckley, J., Byers, K. A., Fake, K., Lehrer, E. W., Tuten, H., & Schell, C. J. (2022). One Health for all: Advancing human and ecosystem health in cities by integrating an environmental justice lens. *Annual Revenue of Ecology, Evolution and Systematics*, *53*, 403–426. https://doi.org/10.1146/annurev-ecolsys-102220-031745

Nibert, D. (2013). *Animal oppression and human violence: Domesecration, capitalism, and global conflict*. Columbia University Press.

Ostrom, E. (2005). *Understanding institutional diversity*. Princeton University Press.

Ostrom, E. (2009). A general framework for analysing sustainability of social-ecological systems. *Science*, *325*(5939), 419–422. https://doi.org/10.1126/science.1172133

Singer, P. (1975). *Animal liberation: A new ethics for our treatment of animals*. Harper and Collins.

Singer, P. (2009). Speciesism and moral status. *Metaphilosophy*, *40*(3–4), 567–581. https://doi.org/10.1111/j.1467-9973.2009.01608.x

United Nations System – Chief Executives Board for Coordination. (2023). *Summary of deliberations United Nations system common principles on future generations*. CEB (2023). https://unsceb.org/sites/default/files/2023-08/United%20Nations%20System%20Common%20Principles%20on%20Future%20Generations.pdf

Weiss Brown, E. (1984). The planetary trust: Conservation & intergenerational equity. *Georgetown University Law Center*, *11*(4), 495–582.

Weiss Brown, E. (1989). *Fairness to future generations: International law, common patrimony, and intergenerational equity*. Transnational Publisher Inc.

Weiss Brown, E. (2008). Climate change, intergenerational equity, and international law. *Vermont Journal of Environmental Law*, *9*, 615–627. https://doi.org/10.1177/00113921211065492

6

ONE HEALTH AND SOCIAL PARTICIPATION: THE ROLE OF TRANSDISCIPLINARITY, MULTISECTORALITY, AND KNOWLEDGE INTEGRATION

ABSTRACT

This chapter examines the One Health (OH) approach through the lens of social participation, emphasizing the central roles of transdisciplinarity, multisectorality, and knowledge integration. Addressing the intertwined challenges linking human, animal, and environmental health requires the active and diverse engagement of social actors. Building on the classical distinction between therapeutic, managerial, and scientific participation, the chapter highlights how OH excludes the therapeutic focus on individual patients while relying heavily on managerial and scientific forms of involvement, which acquire greater complexity when extended to animal and environmental domains. A core argument is that effective OH implementation must transcend multidisciplinarity and interdisciplinarity, advancing toward genuine transdisciplinarity, where academic and non-academic actors collaboratively generate new, holistic knowledge. This becomes operational through multisectorality, understood as coordinated action by sectors beyond health to address broader determinants of well-being. The chapter discusses the Transactive Rationality Model as a conceptual guide for structuring such multisectoral collaboration. Co-creation is presented as the highest expression of this approach, enabling collective creativity and context-sensitive problem-solving while fostering more democratic and inclusive governance. Finally, knowledge integration – supported by systems thinking and design thinking – is identified as essential for navigating OH's complexity and institutionalizing sustainable, cross-sectoral decision-making.

Keywords: Social participation; transdisciplinarity; multisectorality; knowledge integration; co-creation; transactive rationality model; systems and design thinking

INTRODUCTION

This chapter explores the OH approach through the lens of social participation, with a specific focus on transdisciplinarity, multisectorality, and knowledge integration. Central to this discussion is understanding that active, diverse involvement on the part of the social actors is essential to address the complex challenges characterizing the interconnection between human, animal, and environmental health. Specifically, the chapter aims to outline the different levels and modes of participation, illustrating how the integration of perspectives and skills from diverse sectors and disciplines is essential to formulate and implement effective and sustainable solutions in the health and environmental fields. It, therefore, highlights how a transdisciplinary and multisectoral approach, supported by methodologies such as co-creation and design thinking, can overcome traditional "silos" and foster more democratic and inclusive governance in the field of OH.

Specifically, the first section, *(One) Health and Social Participation*, introduces the concept of citizen participation in the health sphere, classifying it into three main types based on the object of involvement: therapeutic involvement, managerial involvement, and scientific involvement. However, the greater complexity of participation in OH is highlighted, given that the outcomes extend beyond the improvement of human healthcare and also embrace animal and environmental health.

The second section, *Speaking About Disciplines: Inter, Multi, or Trans?*, analyzes the different modes of integration between disciplines, which are fundamental for the OH approach, namely, multidisciplinarity (disciplines working in parallel without a profound integration), interdisciplinarity (disciplines combining and integrating concepts and methods to address a common problem), and transdisciplinarity (which goes beyond academic integration, engaging players from outside academia to create new knowledge and holistic approaches). What is then emphasized in this section is that OH requires a genuine transdisciplinary approach.

The section entitled *OH and Multisectorality* explores the concept of multisectorality within OH, defining it as the operational transposition necessary to intervene on the social and environmental determinants of health. It explains that multisectorality is a holistic approach able to address non-clinical aspects (social, environmental, economic) and presents the "Transactive rationality model" and its five key concepts: Define, Design, Relate, Realize, and Capture.

In OH, the highest expression of multisectorality is co-creation, and *Co-creation in OH* introduces it as a methodology that emphasizes collective creativity and collaboration. This section describes how co-creation involves a variety of *stakeholders*, including marginalized populations, to address problems in a collaborative and contextually appropriate manner. Also highlighted is the role co-creation plays in improving the effectiveness and sustainability of OH initiatives.

The concluding section focuses on *Knowledge Integration: Systems Thinking and Design Thinking in OH* as crucial approaches for addressing the complexity of OH.

(ONE) HEALTH AND SOCIAL PARTICIPATION

Citizen participation in the health sphere can take place at different levels. Citizen involvement in healthcare can be explained with particular clarity by starting from the object of the involvement (Maturo, 2024). This is a purely ideal-typical division, as there are frequent overlaps between the three areas. In very simple terms, depending on the object of the involvement, the following typology can be proposed:

- therapeutic involvement;
- managerial involvement;
- scientific involvement.

The first type of involvement is *therapeutic*. Roughly speaking, patients – and in some cases the family caregivers – are socialized into medical discourse, their expertise grows, and shared decisions are sought regarding treatment choices. Satisfaction and compliance are thus improved, as are the efficiency and effectiveness of care, and this results in savings in healthcare expenditure.

Therapeutic involvement is based on the prospect of empowering patients by boosting their health literacy. The idea is that the expert patient can effectively intervene in the management of their condition, thus improving their condition (and also containing costs more effectively). As a result of the rise in chronic illnesses, patients living longer with disabilities, and the exponential increase in healthcare costs, individuals must be encouraged to engage in the management of their own care, and they must be supported in their health choices and in implementing healthy behaviors.

The second type of involvement, *managerial* involvement, regards the possibility for citizens and patients to participate in the planning, organization and management of healthcare services. Essentially, this type of social participation involves meetings between various stakeholders: healthcare managers, patient representatives, associations, non-profit organizations, and trade unions. The idea here is that patients and their families, who are increasingly "competent," since they are ultimately the recipients of the interventions, can provide indications to ensure that these interventions are as appropriate and effective as possible. In summary, in this type of social participation in healthcare, patients make their experience available to the health service, which uses it to establish priorities in the design, delivery, and evaluation of health services. In addition, social participation can also be seen as an "ethical" need for the redistribution of power in terms of direct democracy and deliberative democracy (Maturo, 2024). In many cases, it is a partnership between institutions, social organizations, and citizens that gives rise to management processes based on governance, that is, the methodology of institutional guidance and coordination based on social participation rather than hierarchical direction (Maturo, 2024).

The third type of involvement may sometimes overlap with the approach just described in relation to healthcare management. However, it differs from this approach in its emphasis on the *scientific* aspect. In scientific involvement, the predominant relationship is the one between researchers and patients. In this version, patients or citizens participate in – and in some cases even promote – scientific research. An "extreme" version of citizen and (potential) patient participation in health research is community-based participatory research, proposed, and implemented since the late 1990s by Phil Brown. In political terms, it develops and implements the "popular epidemiology" program (Brown, 2013). In summary, the aim of community-based participatory research is to

> *increase community engagement in research to generate scientific knowledge, improve public trust and understanding of science, inform culturally and socially appropriate intervention methods,*

> *improve public health decisions, and stimulate action. (Brown, 2013, p. 154)*

The most fitting example, however, is probably clinical trials. There are many reasons to involve patients in clinical trials:

> *Patients bring distinct and important perspectives as members of the study team; for example, ensuring the relevance and prioritization of research questions, success and transparency of research activities, identification of opportunities and barriers (...) and dissemination of findings into practice. (Deverka et al., 2018, p. 554)*

For these reasons, today,

> *stakeholders who are the intended end users of research results are expected to participate in the research, which can include designing the study, selecting measures, enhancing subject recruitment, interpreting findings, and/or disseminating study findings. (Frank et al., 2015, p. 1034)*

Indeed, according to Staley et al. (2017),

> *they reported gaining new knowledge from patients and carers, which they recognised as distinct from their textbook knowledge of the condition. They used this learning to change their project designs and their new interventions and devices. They also gained new skills in communicating with patients and carers about the aims and significance of their research. Meeting patients for the first time had a profound impact on some researchers, causing them to change their professional values.(...) The involvement also influenced researchers' priorities and preferences, in terms of what questions to ask and of whom, in their project. (Staley et al., 2017, p. 2)*

The genesis of social participation in clinical research can be traced back to the activism of AIDS patients and HIV-positive individuals in the 1980s (Epstein, 1996). In the 1980s, when the spread of AIDS was at its peak, treatments were virtually non-existent. Patients suffered and died in a dramatic fashion. In addition, the stigma attached to AIDS in those years, and indeed in subsequent years, is well known (Sontag, 1988). The only hope patients had of alleviating their suffering was to be recruited into the clinical trials necessary for the discovery of new drugs and their official approval. Unfortunately, this opportunity was not available to everyone. Since clinical trials had to follow precise, apparently "scientific" sampling designs, many candidates were excluded if they did not fall into specific categories of age, gender, stage of disease, or co-presence of other therapies. Ironically, and tragically, some of those who were admitted were treated with placebos. In addition, research methodologies were slow and progress was scarce.

The bitterness and frustration of patients and HIV-positive individuals had reached intolerable levels, and these people turned from passive patients into fierce activists.[1] These activists were extremely competent. They had carefully studied everything that had been written about AIDS in the major scientific publications: etiology, treatments, experimental methodologies... They were cohesively organized, in possession of expert knowledge and endowed with their own collective identity based on biology; they were, as Rabinow puts it (1996), a *biosociality*. Weakened by the disease but empowered by their expertise, these patient-activists (an interesting oxymoron) proposed/required that pharmaceutical companies and the biomedical establishment abandon placebos in favor of different and faster procedures. Most importantly, they demonstrated the positive value of "historical control groups" (i.e., using previous research results as a control group for numerous studies) and the centrality of an approach based on measuring highly sophisticated biostatistics to compare different drugs at the same time.

Compared to what has just been said about participation in healthcare, participation in OH presents one major difference and many similarities. The major difference is that the OH approach does not target individual human (or non-human) patients. The strengthening of the patient's relationship with the healthcare system and clinical care can, therefore, be excluded from the prerogatives of OH. However, the other two types of participation – managerial participation and scientific participation – remain. Nevertheless, they contain elements of further complexity.

The increased complexity of forms of social participation in OH stems from the fact that potential outcomes are not limited to improving healthcare, nor to intervening on specific social determinants of (human) health. They also embrace interventions to improve animal health and environmental health. This extension of their scope, therefore, requires further strengthening of the interdisciplinary and multisectoral nature of the approach. It also requires a strong component of co-creation and design thinking.

SPEAKING ABOUT DISCIPLINES: INTER, MULTI, OR TRANS?

As should now be clear, the OH approach requires an eclectic organizational and action-oriented effort. The planning of actions and interventions based on an OH vision can only be implemented on the basis of heterogeneous skills, embracing expertise ranging from veterinary medicine to urban planning and including areas such as the sociology of health, microbiology, development economics, ecological studies, and geography, as well as the further specializations comprised within each of those disciplines. In addition to this horizontal eclecticism, OH also requires a vertical integration of roles. Academics can produce a certain type of knowledge, but they also need the perspective of citizens and various stakeholders. Implementing OH interventions requires the participation of multiple figures working at different levels: not only policy levels, but also technical areas. As has long been clear in the field of global health,

> *as social problems are inherently complex and multifaceted, their resolution or amelioration often calls for cross-disciplinary research that integrates perspectives from multiple disciplines and fields. Moreover, the translation of science into new and effective programmes and policies typically requires the creation of partnerships spanning diverse groups, including academic groups, governmental agencies, non-governmental organisations (NGOs), and community groups. (Stokols et al., 2023, p. 4)*

From an OH perspective, the complexity is even greater.

The WHO definition of OH states:

> *The One Health approach promotes collaboration between sectors, professions, and disciplines to improve the health of humans, animals, and ecosystems on an equitable basis....*[2]

But what kind of collaboration is being referred to? How do the various disciplines work together?

There are three modes of integration between disciplines: multidisciplinarity, interdisciplinarity, and transdisciplinarity. They are distinguished by their level of integration:

Multidisciplinary mode: The disciplines work in parallel, each contributing their own knowledge without integration in the true sense of the word. In this "side-by-side" approach, the disciplines collaborate, but each one maintains its own methodologies and perspectives.

Interdisciplinary mode: The disciplines combine, integrating concepts, methods, and perspectives to address a common problem. A bridge is created between disciplines, fostering close dialog and the emergence of new shared understandings.

Transdisciplinary mode: This mode goes beyond the integration of academic disciplines and also brings on board non-academic actors (such as communities, stakeholders, local authorities). A higher level of collaboration is created, in which scientific and experiential knowledge merge to address complex problems in a holistically integrated manner.

In summary, multidisciplinarity moves on to interdisciplinarity, which ultimately evolves into transdisciplinarity, that is, a deeper and more comprehensive coordination and collaboration effort:

> *The underlying goal of these terms is to distinguish between low, moderate, and high levels of interconnectedness or intellectual integration. (Jacobs & Frickel, 2009, p. 45)*

The common words for multidisciplinary, interdisciplinary, and transdisciplinary are:

> *additive, interactive, and holistic, respectively. (Choi & Pak, 2006, p. 351)*

In its mature stage, the OH approach is, therefore, genuinely transdisciplinary. The transdisciplinary model can be considered

> *an integrative process whereby scholars and practitioners from both academic disciplines and non-academic fields work jointly to develop and use novel conceptual and methodological approaches that synthesize and extend discipline-specific perspectives, theories, methods, and translational strategies to yield innovative solutions to particular scientific and societal problems. (Stokols et al., 2023, p. 6)*

TD approaches place an emphasis on the generation of

> *novel, often paradigm-expanding or -creating, conceptual frameworks, hypotheses, research designs, and translations of scientific outcomes into solutions to social problems. (Stokols et al., 2023, p. 6)*

The foregoing can be summarized as follows:

Multidisciplinary approach.

- *Definition*: Different professionals from different disciplines work together symbolically or in parallel, maintaining their own specific skills and approaches.
- *Characteristic*: They collaborate without fully integrating their knowledge, respecting disciplinary boundaries.
- *Example*: A team of doctors, nurses, and physiotherapists who simultaneously care for a patient but work separately.

Interdisciplinary approach.

- *Definition*: Disciplines actively integrate to address a common problem, sharing methods and concepts.
- *Characteristic*: Connections are created between disciplines, with a process involving the comparison and integration of knowledge.
- *Example*: A team of professionals who develop a shared care plan, combining different techniques and models to achieve a more complete result.

Transdisciplinary approach.

- *Definition*: The boundaries between disciplines are overcome, creating new shared knowledge and approaches, with a more global and integrated perspective.
- *Characteristic*: New models, tools, and knowledge are developed that go beyond and transcend individual disciplines.
- *Example*: A research or intervention project that combines clinical, social, environmental, and cultural aspects, giving rise to an innovative and shared model.

For a summary, see Table 3.

In addition to content, transdisciplinary approaches may make three crucial contributions to societal transformations:

> *First, they create social contexts for successful knowledge integration, even where such contexts do not occur naturally. Second, as a result of their collaborative and interactive nature,*

Table 3. Integration Between Disciplines.

Type of Approach	Main Characteristics	Practical Example (Health/ Environmental)
Multidisciplinary	Different professionals, parallel work	Different specialists assess a patient without communicating much with each other
Interdisciplinary	Active collaboration, integration	Professionals create a shared care plan
Transdisciplinary	Overcoming disciplinary boundaries, creating new knowledge	OH project integrating clinical, environmental (plants and animals), and social aspects

> *they tend to produce knowledge that is generally perceived as credible, legitimate and salient. Finally, by fostering collaboration among societal and scientific partners, they can build trust and networks that are independent of any hierarchical chains of command. (Hitziger, 2018, p. 212)*

Moreover, the developmental processes of transdisciplinary teams are likely to benefit when members include not only scientists but also professionals and members of local stakeholder groups – including practitioners, policymakers, and citizens – who represent several spheres of community practice and whose diverse perspectives can enrich the development of translational applications to particular community problems (Aboelela et al., 2007).

For this reason, in addition to integration between disciplines, OH requires integration between sectors and policies. It should also be emphasized that OH interventions are not focused (solely) on improving human health through the recognition of the interdependence of human health, animal health, and environmental health, but on improving all three of these dimensions.

OH AND MULTISECTORALITY

In the field of human health, the multisectoral nature of interventions has been theorized since before 2000:

> *The 1997 WHO Conference on Intersectoral Action for Health: a cornerstone for Health-for-All in the Twenty-First Century in Halifax, Canada illustrated the increasing focus on environmental change and its impact on health, which has continued to gain momentum and expand. The Commission on the Social Determinants of Health clarified beyond doubt the determinants of health, health equity and well-being that required action if health is to be improved. Advancing intersectoral coherence in policy-making and action (including for economic policy negotiations and commercial interests) and Health Equity in All Policies was one of the main recommendations of the final report of the Commission in 2008. (WHO, 2018, p. 9)*

Multisectorality in the field of (human) health is the operational response to the need to act upon the social determinants of health. If we recognize that health is strongly influenced by non-clinical, social, environmental, and economic factors, it becomes clear that attempts to change their influence on people – that is, to mitigate their negative effects and enhance their positive effects – require a holistic, integrated, and multisectoral approach:

> *Multisectoral action for health is defined as actions undertaken by non-health sectors, possibly but not necessarily in collaboration with the health sector, on health or on the determinants of health or health equity. (Tangcharoensathien et al., 2017, p. 359)*

Consideration must be given to barriers to, and enablers of, a multisectoral approach:

> *There may be implementation challenges at an institutional level or conflicts of cultural values, while enablers may include equity by design across sectors in how problems are approached, or consideration of what equitable outcomes would look like. We must avoid using a deficit model in working with non-academic groups, in which "recipients" of knowledge are characterised as ignorant or lacking in some way. Indeed, underrepresented knowledges, such as those of children or animals, can help us sidestep tensions within existing power structures. (SAPEA, 2024, p. 31)*

In a highly regarded article published in *the British Medical Journal*, Kuruvilla et al. (2018) present findings across 12 country case studies of multisectoral collaboration, showing how diverse sectors intentionally shape new ways of collaborating and learning, using "business not as usual" strategies to transform situations and achieve shared goals. The results of the case studies and an analytical literature review can be summarized in the "Transactive rationality model." According to this model, inspired by the theories of the American philosopher John Dewey, multisectorality is based on five concepts: Define; Design; Relate; Realize; Capture success. A summary of these concepts is provided below (Fig. 3).

As we can see, a multisectoral approach is also – or should also be – a transdisciplinary approach. Tautologically speaking, it contemplates the participation and coordination of different stakeholders. It also involves the participation of "expert citizens." Clearly, in the case of OH, a multisectoral approach is necessary, given that we are dealing with not one, but three spheres of health:

> *public health threats are complex, and solutions to them are also complex, since the relationship between human health and biodiversity and consequently land-use changes are complex, numerous, and often dispersed in space and time. (Sanga et al., 2024, p. 27)*

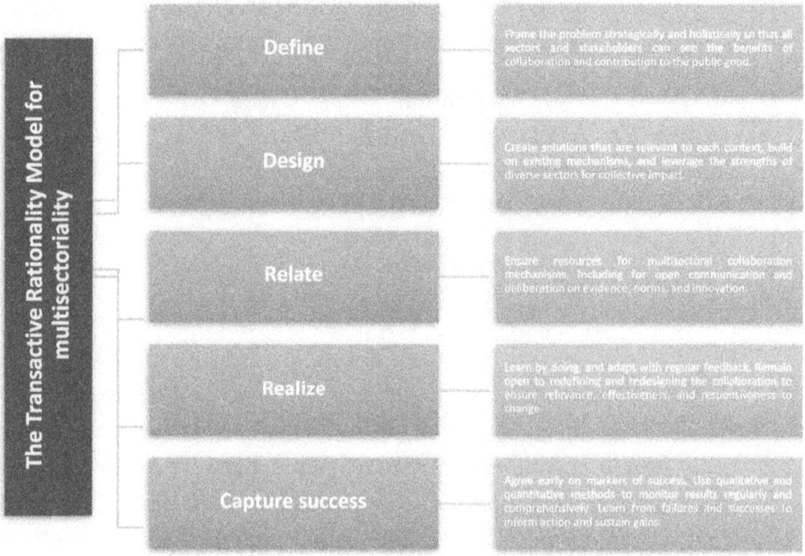

Fig. 3. The Transactive Rationality Model for Multisectoriality.

Given that the transmission of zoonotic diseases is escalating and that human activities such as farming, hunting, mining, and agriculture are among the important social determinants of disease spread,

> *global, regional, and national public health measures require multisectoral action to improve early detection, prevention preparedness, and response to emerging health problems. (Sanga et al., 2024, p. 27)*

CO-CREATION IN OH

Co-creation is a broad methodology that emphasizes collective creativity and collaboration. More specifically:

> *co-creation methods encompass a diverse range of tools, activities, approaches, and techniques strategically employed across the entirety of the co-creation process. These methods serve various purposes, including but not limited to data collection, facilitation, recruitment, reflection, data analysis, and dissemination, allowing for flexibility in achieving diverse objectives. (Agnello et al., 2024, p. 2)*

To be precise, co-creation is the general methodological approach, comprised within which are a series of specific techniques such as Living Labs, Nominal Group Technique, World Café, and Open Space Technology.

In practice, in order to gather diverse opinions, co-creation

> *engages diverse stakeholders, including marginalized populations, in collaborative problem-solving to enhance engagement and develop contextually appropriate solutions. It is increasingly recognized as a way to democratize research and improve the impact of interventions, services, and policies. (Agnello et al., 2025, p. 1)*

It holds promise for enhancing stakeholder engagement, ensuring interventions are tailored to specific needs and contexts, thereby enhancing their relevance, acceptance, and effectiveness. Unlike traditional top-down or bottom-up processes, co-creation adopts a multi-directional approach to problem-solving and fosters democratic processes and knowledge production.

As mentioned, co-creation is increasingly thought of as a methodology to make research and service design more inclusive and diverse and aspires to create a collaboration able to recognize shared insights, work equitably, and share power. For this reason, co-creation envisages and reinforces community engagement:

> *Community engagement as a whole is a strategic approach for collaborative working, targeting a society's community stakeholders for the building of solid relationships and enhancing communication, in order to attain specific goals for the society. The overall focus of Community Engagement in OH research is to enhance the community's aptness in addressing specific health challenges while pointing out these health problems to major stakeholders in research within the community. (Sangong et al., 2025, p. 2)*

Co-creation is a key element for the successful implementation of OH, because it should facilitate collaborations that transcend disciplinary and cultural silos to generate new knowledge and innovative methodologies. This process is vital for OH, because it integrates knowledge from academic and non-academic stakeholders, promoting a transdisciplinary approach, as mentioned above. In terms of efficacy, co-creation enhances the impact and sustainability of OH initiatives, ensuring that interventions are tailored to specific contexts, thus improving their relevance and acceptance. Furthermore, co-creation plays a crucial role in promoting equity and inclusivity, redistributing power and amplifying the voices of participants. This process should enable stakeholders to shape initiatives according to their needs and aspirations, thus fostering trust.

With regard to limitations, the biggest challenge is to promote meaningful and equitable collaboration among the vast diversity of stakeholders. As mentioned, there are difficulties in moving beyond the professional and cultural "silos" that hinder the generation of new knowledge, not to mention the power dynamics in existence between sectors (for instance, the fact that human medicine has historically received more robust funding than public and veterinary health). Other, even more sensitive issues regard the fact that co-creation procedures can generate demands for a strong commitment on the part of the institutions. We live in times when unrealistic claims and demands on the institutions are regularly fueled by populist political positions. There are also other risks, first and foremost, the representativeness of competent citizens: it is often the most vocal – and not necessarily the most competent – individuals that attract the attention of the institutions. Second, the way in which procedures are structured can influence the decision-making process (simply put, control of agenda setting, and therefore the selection of topics to be discussed, define the course of discussion in advance). Furthermore, regarding the results and decisions that arise from discussion/deliberation, it is necessary to consider the extent to which the institution's original plans have influenced the final outcome. Finally, and crucially, emphasizing the democratic nature of the process of involvement and selection of interventions can remove responsibility from the institution, and it is important to distinguish between the contribution of the competent citizen and the responsibility of the institution in carrying out its tasks.

KNOWLEDGE INTEGRATION: SYSTEMS THINKING AND DESIGN THINKING IN OH

Somewhat philosophical though it may sound, we know that the way a problem is framed will determine its boundaries. In other words, things are shaped by the way in which we think about them. In the context of OH, this philosophical assumption is even more true. After all, it would be rather contradictory to argue for the importance of the interconnection between the animal, environmental, and human dimensions without an intrinsically holistic and systemic vision, and in effect, system thinking:

> *focuses on the holistic perspective of a system, and the observed behaviours that emerge from the interactions between the parts of the system. (Thelen et al., 2023, p. 2)*

The origins of this conception of reality lie in the systems theory developed in the 1940s, the main concepts of which included holism, but also feedback, homeostasis, multifinality, and equifinality. This orientation subsequently gave rise to a current of study focused on complexity. This orientation is particularly akin to the OH approach:

> *Systems Science is a transdisciplinary approach that deals with the complexity of natural, social and other systems. Treating One Health together with its subsystems (ecosystem, people and animal health) as a complex system within the Systems Science concept opens doors for finding answers on how interventions (Systems Design) can generate a sustainable change in One Health outcomes. (Burger, 2024, p. 1)*

At both a theoretical and operational level, there is no clear idea of how genuine governance based on the OH approach can be implemented. However, it is fairly evident that knowledge integration at every stage of policy development can be the starting point for OH governance. As we shall see, this perspective can be supported through the very concepts of systems theory, or rather, the evolution of the theory.

Although some forms of knowledge integration from different disciplines, institutions, and sectors can – and already do – occur intuitively, in many circumstances, it is important that they become institutionalized at project, program, and, indeed, policy level.

In its broadest sense, knowledge integration has been defined as the construction of shared and meaningful syntheses between distinct mental models (Hitziger et al., 2018). This integration has been compared to interweaving multiple perspectives into a central vision or to the search for coherence and correspondence (Hitziger et al., 2018). Promoting effective knowledge integration in a policy cycle is a multidimensional challenge, because it requires the integration of heterogeneous organizational interests and perspectives, which are also characterized by different communication codes and cultural roots. The key to integrating knowledge is an understanding of how different actors can have interests, preferences, and values that are often in conflict with one another. It is, therefore, a question of developing mediation and negotiation strategies to achieve integrated collective action. This objective can be achieved through multi-criteria analysis, but above all the adoption of design thinking practices. Multi-criteria analyses can support such integration because they elicit and structure value systems in order to accommodate multiple, heterogeneous sources and types of information as an information base.

The support of design thinking, as a means of integrating knowledge, is perfectly consistent with a transdisciplinary and multisectoral approach:

> *Increasingly, dynamic perspectives that explore how issues within subsystems (e.g., the separate human, animal, and environmental dimensions) influence one another within a complete system require so-called "systems-thinking approaches." Such approaches need to use and understand multisectoral information using multidisciplinary, interdisciplinary, and trans-disciplinary methods to inform outputs describing a spectrum of possible outcomes. (Arnold et al., 2024, pp. 124–125)*

Design thinking is a creative design style that can be used to identify innovative solutions focused on the user and their needs (Xie et al., 2017). The stages of design thinking can be roughly listed as follows:

- *Understand, explore, and empathize*: in-depth social analysis of the context and thorough exploration of the needs, desires, and expectations of the participants;
- *Define*: synthesizing all the data collected and laying the foundations for a design that is truly focused on the analysis context;
- *Ideate*: broadening the perspective and creating as many solutions as possible until a satisfactory result is achieved;
- *Prototype*: creating a possible model of the solution;
- *Test*: submitting the solution to the participants for their opinion. This will enable strengths and weaknesses to emerge at an early stage, significantly facilitating corrections.

Once the design thinking cycle has been completed, the outcome should be subjected to further forms of validation and evaluation.

Burger (2024) seeks to provide a comprehensive picture of the use of system thinking in OH by adding the two techniques of systems dynamics and systems design (effectively design thinking). Moving from epistemology, that is, the most abstract way of knowing, to forms of empirical knowledge, and on to techniques, the progress of research and intervention in an OH perspective can be depicted as follows:

> *One Health Systems Science can address complex challenges via Systems Thinking – identifying interdependent components and adaptive agents, Systems Dynamics – understanding the structure*

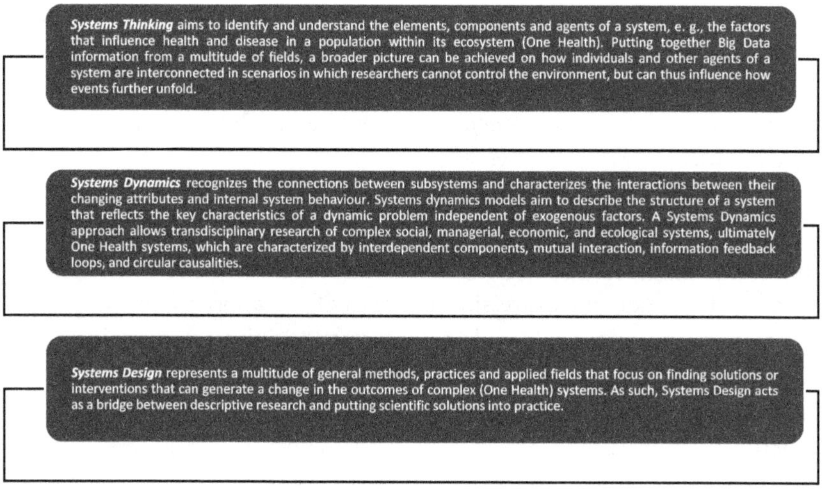

Fig. 4. Knowledge Integration Model.

> *and connectivity within and between components, and Systems Design – finding solutions for sustainable change. (Burger, 2024, p. 3)*

The foregoing can be summarized in Fig. 4.

IN A NUTSHELL…

In summary, in this chapter, we have argued that OH approach, viewed through the lens of social participation, requires the active and diverse involvement of the social actors. This is crucial for addressing the complex challenges arising from the interconnection between human, animal, and environmental health. The key take-home message is that the achievement of effective and sustainable solutions in OH necessarily requires the adoption of methodologies that promote knowledge integration, multisectoral collaboration, and the overcoming of disciplinary boundaries.

With regard to the social participation of citizens in healthcare, in the OH context, the strengthening of the direct relationship between individual human patients and clinical care (therapeutic involvement) is excluded, but social participation of a managerial and scientific nature remains essential. The OH field, which aims to improve human, animal, and environmental health, introduces greater complexity than individual human health, that is, the focus on the patient.

To manage this complexity, OH requires an authentic transdisciplinary approach, one that is able to move beyond multidisciplinarity and interdisciplinarity. Transdisciplinarity surpasses academic integration, bringing on board non-academic actors (such as communities and stakeholders) to create new knowledge and innovative solutions.

The OH approach is implemented operationally through multisectorality, defined as the action taken by sectors (social, environmental, economic) that are not strictly related to health in order to intervene on health determinants. In OH, the maximum expression of this holistic approach is co-creation. Co-creation is a methodology that stimulates collective creativity in a structured manner and involves a variety of stakeholders, including vulnerable social groups, to develop context-appropriate solutions. It is central to the practical implementation of OH, because it enables genuinely eclectic action that goes beyond cultural and institutional silos, with a strong impact and sustainability. We have of course highlighted potential critical issues and risks that may arise at the practical implementation stage.

One model for multisectoral collaboration is the "Transactive Rationality Model," based on five key concepts: *Define, Design, Relate, Realize, Capture*. Furthermore, OH governance requires the integration of knowledge at every stage of policy development, which can be achieved through systems thinking and design thinking. The integration of knowledge, supported by a transdisciplinary and multisectoral approach, is the key to finding sustainable solutions for change in OH.

We hope to have coherently argued that the success of OH lies not only in the blend of academic expertise required, but in the ability to institutionalize the integration of knowledge between different worlds (disciplinary, sectoral, and community) in order to shape and implement policies and interventions in a way that is both inclusive and effective.

NOTES

1. We refer to Vanessa Heggle's article published in The Guardian, *World AIDS Day. How AIDS Activists Changed Medical Research,* 1 December 2013. Available at: https://www.theguardian.com/science/2013/dec/01/world-aids-day-how-aids-activists-changed-medical-research.

2. See https://www.who.int/health-topics/one-health#tab=tab_1.

REFERENCES

Aboelela, S. W., Larson, E., Bakken, S., Carrasquillo, O., Formicola, A., Glied, S. A., Haas, J., & Gebbie, K. M. (2007). Defining interdisciplinary research: Conclusions from a critical review of the literature. *Health Services Research*, *42*(1), 329–346. https://doi.org/10.1111/j.1475-6773.2006.00621.x

Agnello, D. M., Anand-Kumar, V., An, Q., Boer, D. J., Delfmann, L. R., Longworth, G. R., Loisel, Q., McCaffrey, L., Steiner, A., & Chastin, S. (2025). Co-creation methods for public health research – Characteristics, benefits, and challenges: A Health CASCADE scoping review. *BMC Medical Research Methodology*, *25*(1), 60. https://doi.org/10.1186/s12874-025-02514-4

Agnello, D. M., Balaskas, G., Steiner, A., & Chastin, S. (2024). Methods used in co-creation within the health CASCADE co-creation database and grey literature: Systematic methods overview. *Interactive Journal of Medical Research*, *13*, e59772. https://doi.org/10.2196/59772

Arnold, K. E., Laing, G., McMahon, B. J., Fanning, S., Stekel, D. J., Pahl, O., Coyne, l., Latham, S. M., McIntyre, M. K., & McIntyre, K. M. (2024). The need for One Health systems – Thinking approaches to understand multiscale dissemination of antimicrobial resistance, *Lancet Planet Health*, *8*(2), e124–e133. https://doi.org/10.1016/S2542-5196(23)00278-4

Brown, P. (2013). Integrating medical and environmental sociology with environmental health: Crossing boundaries and building connections through advocacy. *Journal of Health and Social Behavior*, *54*(2), 145–164. https://doi.org/10.1177/0022146513484473

Burger, P. A. (2024). Integrating One Health into systems science. *One Health*, *18*, 1–3. https://doi.org/10.1016/j.onehlt.2024.100701

Choi, B. C., & Pak, A. W. (2006). Multidisciplinarity, interdisciplinarity and transdisciplinarity in health research, services, education and policy: 1. Definitions, objectives, and evidence of effectiveness. *Clinical and Investigative Medicine*, *29*(6), 351–364.

Deverka, P. A., Bangs, R., Kreizenbeck, K., Delaney, D. M., Hershman, D. L., Blanke, C. D., & Ramsey, S. D. (2018). A new framework for patient engagement in cancer clinical trials cooperative group studies. *Journal of National Cancer Institute*, *110*(6), 553–559. https://doi.org/10.1093/jnci/djy064

Epstein, S. (1996). *Impure science: AIDS, activism, and the politics of knowledge*. University of California Press.

Frank, L., Forsythe, L., Ellis, L., Schrandt, S., Sheridan, S., Jason Gerson, J., Konopka, K., & Daugherty S. (2015). Conceptual and practical foundations of patient engagement in research at the patient-centred outcomes research institute. *Quality of Life Research*, *24*(5), 1033–1041. https://doi.org/10.1007/s11136-014-0893-3

Hitziger, M., Esposito, R., Canali, M., Aragrande, M., Häsler, B., & Rüegg, S. R. (2018). Knowledge integration in One Health policy formulation, implementation and evaluation. *Bulletin of the World Health Organization*, *96*(3), 211–218. https://doi.org/10.2471/BLT.17.202705

Jacobs, J. A., & Frickel, S. (2009). Interdisciplinarity: A critical assessment. *Annual Review of Sociology*, *35*(1), 43–65.

Kuruvilla, S., Hinton, R., Boerma, T., Bunney, R., Casamitjana, N., Cortez, R., Fracassi, P., Franz-Vasdeki, J., Helldén, D., McManus, J., Papp, S., Rasanathan, K., Requejo, J., Silver, K. L., Tenhoope-Bender, P., Velleman, Y., Wegner, M . N., Armstrong, C . E., Barnett, S., ... Graham, W. (2018). Business not as usual: How multisectoral collaboration can promote transformative change for health and sustainable development. *BMJ*, *363*, k4771. https://doi.org/10.1136/bmj.k4771

Maturo, A. (2024). *Il primo libro di sociologia della salute*. Einaudi.

Rabinow, P. (1996). Artificiality and enlightenment: From sociobiology to biosociality. In P. Rabinow (Ed.), *Essays on the anthropology of reason*. Princeton University Press.

Sanga, V. T., Karimuribo, E. D., & Hoza, A. S. (2024). One Health in practice: Benefits and challenges of multisectoral coordination and collaboration in managing public health risks: A meta-analysis. *International Journal of One Health*, *10*(1), 26–36. https://doi.org/10.14202/IJOH.2024.26-36

Sangong, S., Saah, F. I., & Bain, L. E. (2025). Effective community engagement in one health research in Sub-Saharan Africa: A systematic review. *One Health Outlook*, 7(4), 1–15. https://doi.org/10.1186/s42522-024-00126-4

SAPEA. (2024). *One Health governance in the European Union*. SAPEA. https://zenodo.org/records/14055991

Sontag, S. (1988). *Aids and its metaphors*. farrar.straus and giroux

Staley, K., Abbey-Vital, I., & Nolan, C. (2017). The impact of involvement on researchers: A learning experience. *Research Involvement & Engagement*, *3*(20). https://doi.org/10.1186/s40900-017-0071-1

Stokols, D., Hall, K. L., & Vogel, A. L. (2023). Transdisciplinary public health. Definitions, core characteristics and strategies for success. In D. Haire-Joshu & T. D. McBride (Eds.), *Transdisciplinary public health: Research, methods and practice* (pp. 3–30). Jossey-Bass.

Tangcharoensathien, V., Srisookwatana, O., Pinprateep, P., Posayanonda, T., & Patcharanarumol, W. (2017). Multisectoral actions for health: Challenges and opportunities in complex policy environments. *International Journal of Health Policy and Management*, *6*(7), 359–363. https://doi.org/10.15171/ijhpm.2017.61

Thelen, J., Sant Fruchtman, C., Bilal, M., Gabaake, K., Iqbal, S., Keakabetse, T., Kwamie, K., Mokalake, E., Mupara, L . M., Seitio-Kgokgwe, O., Zafar, S., Daniel Cobos Muñoz, D. S., & Munoz, D. C. (2023). Development of the systems thinking for health actions framework: A literature review and a case study. *BMJ Global Health*, *8*, e010191. https://doi.org/10.1136/bmjgh-2022-010191

WHO. (2018). *Health in all policies as part of the primary health care agenda on multisectoral action, Technical Series on Primary Care*. 1–28. https://www.who.int/publications/i/item/WHO-HIS-SDS-2018.59

Xie, T., Liu, W., Anderson, B. D., Liu, X., & Gray, G. C. (2017). A system dynamics approach to understanding the One Health concept. *PLoS One*, *12*(9), e0184430. https://doi.org/10.1371/journal.pone.0184430

UNCLUSIONS. SOCIOLOGY FOR OH: BETWEEN THEORY AND PRACTICE

In this final chapter, I will be making two proposals. The first concerns the relationship between OH and sociological knowledge. I will propose three characteristics of OH that in my opinion make this perspective entirely unique and original, when viewed through a sociological framework. The second proposal concerns the areas of OH in which the sociological approach can be used at an operational level.

The first case regards areas we have already discussed in many parts of this work, but I believe it is also useful to look at them separately. These three areas share a certain complexity. The first characteristic is *interdependence*. In terms of both cognitive analysis and practical action, this area requires a transdisciplinary and multisectoral approach. The second characteristic of OH is the plurality of the dimensions of *equity and justice* it is made up of: in addition to the dimensions of environmental justice, interspecies justice, and social justice, it embraces intergenerational justice (which is a component of sustainability) and epistemic justice (important in OH for ignored knowledge and social participation). Furthermore, these dimensions of justice are interdependent. The third point is an invitation to explore the notion of *exposome*. From an anthropocentric perspective, the exposome coincides with the set of exposures that affect our health: environmental exposures (e.g., pollution), behavioral and social exposures (e.g., lifestyles), internal exposures (e.g., hormonal processes). In some areas, not only of science, but also of insurance (!), attempts are made to quantify these exposures in order to predict people's risk of disease. My proposal is to "rotate" the elements of the exposome, considering, for example, the environment as the center of the system and looking at its exposures in relation to human activities and human effects on the environment. Animals also have an effect on the environment: think, for instance, of the rumination of cows and the effect it has on global warming. The same can be done by focusing on animal health.

Animal health is exposed to climate change (environment), and it is also affected by wars (humans). Unfortunately, humans are often the source of many environmental and animal health problems (and also of problems that affect their own health).

The second proposal concerns three areas in which sociology can have an immediate practical application. The first area is critical thinking. The sociology of health shows how social inequality is the fundamental cause of disease and thus invites us, in a sense, to take a broader view than that of biomedicine. Similarly, in the field of OH, sociology can reveal many aspects that are taken for granted but are oppressive. And on this point, we can again see the different types of justice and the sociology of ignorance. This critical function is not only theoretical: it can also be pursued through empirical research. There is nothing more concrete than a good theory.

The second area regards social research methodologies. Focus groups, living labs, and creative methods can play an important role in many phases of OH interventions. They can be used during the information gathering phase and the dissemination phase, and above all, some of these methodologies are indispensable for increasing community involvement with a view to co-creation.

The third area of sociological investment once again regards sociological methodology. However, these are sociological methods for prediction. Sociological methodology can play a central role in predicting ecological and pandemic disasters within the context of OH.

INTERDEPENDENCE

Interdependence is a long-recognized principle in public health:

> *Interdependence involves achieving community health in a way that respects individual rights, while recognising that the health of some often depends on the health of others. (Meagher, 2024; Swain et al., 2008, p. 354).*

This vision also underpins the research program of Christakis and Fowler (2009). The two demonstrate how "I gain weight if my friend's friend gains weight." In other words, Christakis and Fowler (2009) show the power of networks and, in short, how innovations and behaviors – quitting smoking, getting divorced, gaining weight – spread among interconnected people, even those who are several degrees of separation apart.

More recently, in 2019, the American Public Health Association proposed a definition of interdependence that is very much in line with OH:

> *The health of every individual is linked to the health of every other individual within the human community, to other living creatures, and to the integrity and functioning of environmental ecosystems. Public health practitioners and organizations have an ethical obligation to foster positive – and mitigate negative – relationships among individuals, societies, and environments in ways that protect and promote the flourishing of humans, communities, nonhuman animals, and the ecologies in which they live. (American Public Health Association, 2019)*

"Inter" – Latin for "between" – is a recurring prefix in One Health, found in terms such as interdependence, interdisciplinarity, interspeciesism, intergenerationality, or intersectorality. The proliferation of these terms invites us to see health in OH as something relational, not as a clearly defined entity that can be found and definitively measured in someone or something. In OH, health is expressed in relationships and is a property of relationships; indeed, it is their main property, from an ethical and normative perspective. If relationships are healthy, then the entities that these relationships bind will also be healthy. However, if we look even closer, we discover that what we thought were monolithic entities are in fact nothing more than other systems, apparatuses, organizations that are also made up of relationships between entities, which if we look even closer…

If we consider that humans and animals form an interdependent multispecies collective together with the manifold organisms that populate their bodies, this also requires a rethink of the concept of the individual, the entity *par excellence*:

> *if microbes are an interdependent (not just a merely interconnected) part of who we are, then any attempt to unwillingly alter our microbiome might well be considered a personal assault rather than a mere modification of our environmental conditions. Changing the ways we think about how things are related (biologically) invites us to reconsider our value conceptions and the value priorities that orient us, ethically, to problems of health and the methods by which those values are enacted. (Beever & Morar, 2019, p. 186)*

Let us go down to a less abstract level and see, once again – but from a different perspective (the passage is taken from an article that appeared in a veterinary science journal) – why OH should be based on the principle of interdependence:

> *The need to respond to emerging infectious diseases required an acknowledgment that human health is interdependent with the natural world at large. Zoonotic diseases, with the majority finding their source in wildlife, have pressed upon health professionals the recognition that human health is vulnerable to disease outbreaks at the wildlife-interface. Moreover, anthropogenic impact on the environment represents a significant driver in the emergence of such diseases, making humans both vulnerable as well as implicated in the rise of emerging zoonoses. (Nieuwland & Meijboom, 2020, pp. 4–5)*

At this point, it should be clear that there is a difference between interconnectedness and interdependence. Interconnectedness describes a set of causal relations. For example, unhealthy pollutants entering the water stream cause the pollution of the river. Unlike a story of simple cause and effect, interdependence captures a qualitatively distinct mode of determination that is mutually dependent:

> *The mutual dependence condition shows that the nature of the relations between an object and some environmental conditions is more than merely causal when those external factors are reliably integrated into the nature of the whole. This condition highlights that not all interactions are of equal importance for an object (as the interconnectedness view seems to assume). This aspect is crucial not only from an epistemic perspective because it pinpoints constitutive interactions between an organism and its environment, but it also defines – even if sometimes only loosely – a significant moral threshold to which we should be differently sensitive. (Beever & Morar, 2020, p. 21)*

However, interdependence is not just a *horizontal* issue of complex causal relationships between different parties, even across many degrees of separation. Interdependence has a *lean* dimension, given that it is complex, that is, it consists of threshold effects, feedback loops, equifinality, and multicausality. Perhaps less obviously, however, interdependence is also *vertical*: the decisions we make today have long-term effects on future generations and, conversely, the final states we imagine will characterize the future, the present futures, interact with the present, and influence the decisions we make today. We discussed this in the chapter on the future, but without linking it to the idea of interdependence. Furthermore, if we combine interdependence + future, we inevitably touch on the themes of another of our chapters: the one on justice. A very clear example can be offered:

> *Like climate change, antimicrobial resistance heightens the importance of time in our moral and political deliberations. The rise of pathogens that can resist treatment highlights intergenerational justice: what we (fail to) do now to conserve antimicrobial effectiveness determines the infectious disease burden borne by those in the future. (Meagher, 2024, p. 163)*

OH JUSTICE: MULTIPLE CONNECTIONS

This last quote allows us to broaden and apply the discussion on the interdependence and interconnections between the various dimensions of justice that we analyzed in Chapter 5.

In OH, there are multiple relationships between environmental justice and intergenerational justice. The most obvious is the relationship linked to sustainability: intergenerational justice focuses on the need to ensure that future generations can enjoy the same resources and opportunities as the present generations, while environmental justice aims to protect the environment and manage resources sustainably, ensuring that future generations are not penalized by decisions made today. The two are not only interconnected; they overlap. A second example regards vulnerable communities. Vulnerable communities, which are often impacted by environmental injustices, may suffer the most from the negative effects of environmental degradation. These injustices can perpetuate a cycle of inequality that also impacts opportunities for future generations. Many sociological theories, including the "fundamental cause" perspective, clearly explain how inequalities can be perpetuated in vicious circles and can be "inherited" by subsequent generations (Maturo, 2024).

There are also multiple relationships between interspecies justice and intergenerational justice. Notably, there are two ways in which interspecies justice supports intergenerational justice: first, by ensuring the survival and flourishing of other species, interspecies justice helps maintain the ecological stability and biodiversity that future generations will need to thrive; second, protecting ecosystems for the sake of interspecies justice is a form of intergenerational justice, as these ecosystems provide services that future generations will depend on.

At the same time, there are two ways in which intergenerational justice supports interspecies justice: first, just as we have obligations to future humans, intergenerational justice can be seen as having obligations to future non-human life, meaning we must not cause extinctions or irreversible harm that will negatively affect the future of other species; second, the very idea that future generations (including future non-human animals) are entitled to a healthy planet is a foundation for interspecies justice. Since interspecies justice could also be seen as part of environmental justice, or at least as a consequence of it, there are overlaps between these two spheres.

It is important to bear in mind that these reflections on the various types of justice, their interconnections and their interdependencies should not be seen as abstract attempts at philosophical speculation (with all due respect for philosophy). These are not empty theories about justice, and we believe it is important to understand their immediate pragmatic application, summarized effectively by Leonnert Bossert with regard to ecological crises:

> *Emissions from global animal agriculture are fostering climate change, cutting down forests for grazing land and producing animal food crops contributes to biodiversity loss, and keeping many nonhuman animals in (too) confined spaces can lead to outbreaks of zoonotic infectious diseases, which in turn can reach epidemics or pandemics. The same holds true of contact with wild animals when they are traded. The negative consequences of global animal agriculture have been identified by numerous scientists as including high land consumption, massive deforestation, degradation of arable land, consumption of large quantities of freshwater, increased ocean acidification, and pollution of water, air, and soil by manure, hormones, antibiotics, and other "by-products" of animal farming. (Bossert, 2024, p. 1)*

On another level, it can also be noted that sustainable environmental practices, such as consuming organic food, using eco-friendly transport, or adopting green technologies, often require significant economic resources. People with limited means may find these choices difficult to afford. On the other hand, there are hugely polluting consumption patterns that are the prerogative of people with a certain level of spending power (air travel, for instance). Going back to vulnerable communities and consumption patterns, it should be noted that energy policies can sometimes benefit wealthier consumers (e.g., through incentives for the installation of solar panels) more than impoverished communities, creating a gap between those who can benefit from a green economy and those who continue to suffer due to the scarcity of resources.

There are also multiple interdependencies between epistemic injustice and other dimensions of justice. Indeed, from a critical perspective, it can be argued that the entire rhetoric of sustainability is flawed by an original epistemic injustice:

> *Discourses around sustainability and resilience are most often framed in anthropocentric terms, as in sustainable human use and resilience to human disturbance, all with a goal of providing for human societies within the context of perpetual growth and the extractivist logics of capital. (Van Patter, 2023, p. 3)*

This view establishes a precise hierarchy between human and non-human animals and makes oppression and exploitation automatic, or rather "natural." Neoliberalism, with the commodification of animal bodies,

> *transforms the violence perpetrated on sentient beings into procedures to increase production efficiency. (Baquero, 2021, p. 7)*

Taking up the definition of capitalism as "a shared marginalising apparatus" (Baquero et al., 2021, p. 2), Van Patter et al. (2023, p. 3) see reality as

> *a system, or relation, in which humans, other-than-human animals, and the land are all enmeshed within intersecting relations of power. (Van Patter et al., 2023, p. 3)*

Thus, epistemic injustice produces strategic ignorance, that is, gray areas and undone science on all knowledge that can distort or reduce neoliberal efficiency. This knowledge is "marginalized." It is, therefore, no coincidence that Baquero et al. (2021), reflecting on these limitations, call for a "counter-hegemonic ecology of knowledge grounded in global South epistemologies" (Van Patter et al., 2023, p. 3) constituted by seven actions:

> *(1) deconstruct apparatuses of marginalisation; (2) enrich the ecology of knowledge; (3) build healthy multispecies public policy; (4) create supportive environments; (5) strengthen multispecies community actions; (6) develop individual capabilities in multiple species, and (7) reorient multispecies health services. (Baquero et al., 2021, p. 9)*

As we can see, the first two points are directly aimed at redimensioning sources of epistemic injustice.

EXPOSOME AND SOCIO-EXPOSOME

Allow me to digress a little. Once upon a time, way back around 2010, there was a very angry father. The man, visibly agitated, walked into a Target store on the outskirts of Minneapolis. He asked to speak to the manager and when he arrived, the man waved some coupons and discount vouchers in his face...

> *"My daughter got this in the mail!" he said. "She's still in high school, and you're sending her coupons for baby clothes and cribs? Are you trying to encourage her to get pregnant?"*[1]

The manager apologized profusely and stammered that he had no idea how this could have happened.

A few days later, the manager called the father to apologize again, but something happened:

> *On the phone, though, the father was somewhat abashed. "I had a talk with my daughter," he said. "It turns out there's been some activities in my house I haven't been completely aware of. She's due in August. I owe you an apology."*[2]

What had happened was that in the office the Target chain had recently set up, where a mysterious new discipline called *Predictive Analytics* was practiced, a sudden and unexpected change in the young woman's shopping pattern had been noticed, as indicated by her loyalty card. As early as 2010, attempts were already being made to collect even the smallest details about customers' consumption patterns. And at Target, they had noticed that:

> *Women on the baby registry were buying larger quantities of unscented lotion around the beginning of their second trimester. Another analyst noted that sometime in the first 20 weeks, pregnant women loaded up on supplements such as calcium, magnesium and zinc. Many shoppers purchase soap and cotton balls, but when someone suddenly starts buying lots of scent-free soap and extra-large bags of cotton balls, in addition to hand sanitizers and washcloths, it signals that they could be getting close to their delivery date.*[3]

The young woman's pregnancy had thus already become evident in her "data double," even before it became apparent in her social identity.

This happened over 15 years ago, when paper mail was still common. In the meantime, there has been a massive rise in self-tracking, through which we generate enormous amounts of data, especially physiological and behavioral data. In addition, sophisticated algorithms can monitor the time we spend on a website, the physical places we visit, and the likes we give. By monitoring our credit cards, it is possible to know what we eat and how many calories we consume. Especially after COVID-19, sensors that we cannot even see can identify who has a fever at a railway station. In the field of health, therefore, we have not only big data but also *thick data*: "dense" data that can tell us about our health from a clinical, physical, and social point of view (Maturo & Setiffi, 2023). American health insurance companies have a strong interest in collecting health data, as they need to know the state of health of their members: their profits grow if their members make little use of health services. This explains the phenomena, theoretically prohibited, of *adverse selection* and *cream skimming* (trying to avoid members who are likely to fall ill, i.e., essentially the poor).

If the office of a chain store was able to discover a customer's pregnancy through her purchases of hygiene products more than 15 years ago, what can health insurance companies find out about us today when we give them access to our socio-demographic data, clinical data, genetic predispositions, and, above all, data relating to our lifestyles? And by lifestyle data, we don't just mean whether we are smokers or vegetarians, but all our digital activities and our "data doubles." After all, some digital platforms have already identified a substantial set of data points as proxies for our health status:

> *individual purchasing behavior, consumer engagement with advertising, insurance claims, sentiment, and expression in online forums, credit histories, and online social networks. (Rowe, 2021, p. 4)*

In addition, of course, to all the now commonplace data, we collect thanks to our electronic bracelets (often a gift from health insurance companies in the USA). Some health insurance companies actually link the price of the policy to constant digital monitoring of our physical activity. This means that, in theory, the price of the policy could fluctuate every day, rather than once a year.

Since we delved into the past with the story of the father and his pregnant daughter, let's stay in the "old days" a little longer and remember a 1997 film entitled *Gattaca*. Gattaca is set in a near future in which society is divided into two social classes: the Valids and the In-Valids. The Valids are those who have a healthy genetic makeup, the result of embryo selection. The In-Valids are those who were born naturally and, therefore, have imperfections of various types and degrees. Based on genetic testing, it is, therefore, possible to predict people's life expectancy and thus allocate them to more or less prestigious jobs. Obviously, the Valids are at the top of the social ladder and the In-Valids are relegated to the most menial jobs. Thus, in Gattaca, genetic makeup *predicts* an individual's position in society, acting as a factor of social inclusion or exclusion. It is no coincidence that the artistic genre to which Gattaca is ascribed is known as "biopunk."

Today, there are high expectations regarding the *Polygenic Risk Score*, that is, the estimate of the probability of developing a particular medical condition by evaluating information from multiple genetic markers and variants. This approach is very far removed, in terms of accuracy and complexity, from any possibility of "genetic determinism" (Conley & Fletcher, 2017).

Now, what if we could also develop scores regarding social factors? In other words, is it possible to estimate the effect on a person's physiology of their level of education, income, family status, lifestyle, social networks, and consumption patterns? As the story of the father – or rather the grandfather – mentioned earlier shows, the answer is yes. In some areas of American academic research, work is under way to develop the *Polysocial Risk Score* – an index that quantifies our risk of illness based on social factors (Figueroa et al., 2020; Maturo, 2022). This is not unexpected news: after all, if we have the *genome* and *biomarkers*, why can't we analyze and study the *exposome*? And why not identify, weigh and codify something that can be defined as a *sociomarker*?

Epidemiologists and sociologists have produced a huge amount of quantitative research on the relationship between social determinants and health. This research is often very sophisticated, allowing us to estimate the impact of education on the ability to quit smoking, or the relationship between neighborhood of residence and being vegan; it can show that among people of high social status there are few teetotalers but also very few heavy drinkers. These are just a few examples. A classic study argues that:

> *using the best available estimates, the impacts of various domains on early deaths in the U.S. distribute roughly as follows: genetic predispositions, about 30%; social circumstances, 15%; environmental exposures, 5%; behavioral patterns, 40%; and shortfalls in medical care, 10%. (McGinnis et al., 2002, p. 83).*

Of these dimensions, at least social circumstances, lifestyle and behavioral patterns, and environmental exposure can be partly incorporated into the concept of the exposome.

The exposome can be described based on three axes: general external environment, specific external environment, and internal environment

(Wild, 2005). The general external environment includes factors such as climate and urbanization, which can be measured at population level; the specific external environment, such as diet or smoking habits, can be measured at individual level using questionnaires, environmental sensors, or personal dosimeters; the internal environment includes hormonal, inflammatory, and molecular processes, measured as a whole using high-throughput "omic" methods, aimed at providing a comprehensive description of the set of molecules in a biological system (e.g., proteome, transcriptome, metabolome). In summary, the exposome encompasses and identifies the set of "exposures" an individual is subjected to during their lifetime. Some are eminently subjective, although socially conditioned (e.g., smoking), while others are more contextual and less avoidable (e.g., environmental pollution). On a broader level, with regard to science policy, it is necessary to reflect on the possible evolution of this promising, if not revolutionary, area of study:

> *Exposome research could proceed along one of two paths – it could either follow the path of the genome and take a radically individualized turn (towards so-called personalized medicine initiatives), or, more optimistically, it could produce a more holistic and multilayered assessment of social, political, economic environments and how they interact to influence health. (Senier et al., 2016, p. 107)*

From these considerations, we can see that there are opportunities, and therefore, discussions, about the role of the exposome in human health, and numerous reflections can undoubtedly be made along the axis of social justice.

The discussion can also be extended to OH, and there have been many attempts and proposals to integrate OH and exposome (Gao, 2021; Ibanez et al., 2024; Matus et al., 2024). However, these proposals appear to be geared toward using this integration to enhance public health interventions. In summary:

> *This innovative approach enables tailored interventions, disease outbreak predictions, and a holistic understanding of the intricate links between human health and the environment, offering substantial benefits for public health and disease prevention despite existing challenges. (Matus et al., 2024, p. 1)*

Therefore, even though the OH approach is included, the ultimate beneficiaries of the health gains made possible through this mixed perspective are still individuals. In other words, anthropocentrism persists even with OH approaches.

There is another possible path, which would involve conceiving and rotating the systems – human, environmental, animal – that make up OH, central to the configuration of the exposome. This path would allow us to place animals at the center and assess and quantify the role of the environment in their health (e.g., the implications of pollution and deforestation for animals), as well as to assess how human activities (such as wars) affect animals.

The other step is to place the environment at the center of the configuration and thus consider "the environment of the environment," that is, what humans do to nature (and unfortunately, we already know a lot about this), and how animals affect the environment (e.g., emissions from cows, waste from intensive farming).

This is, therefore, a mental experiment in dislocation: removing humans from the center of the exposome (just for a while) and seeing what happens if we put the environment and animals in their place. It is a serious experiment, however, and one that can help us see things from different perspectives. The One Health Perspective.

THREE AREAS OF WORK FOR SOCIOLOGY

Sociology can strengthen the OH perspective in at least three ways. These contributions extend beyond the sociology of health and have already been explored in depth in this work.

The first contribution regards the critical perspective. Sociology can show that many institutions, social organizations, and belief systems originate from a certain socio-economic context and are functional to its preservation. Multiple cultural aspects, from a certain type of language to particular forms of institutional organization, are linked to specific structural forces and power configurations of a particular moment in history.

The critical approach in health sociology shows how the biomedical system and medical dominance have reduced attention to the importance of social factors in health. The concept of "structural violence" illuminates the ways in which inequalities, stigma, and medicalization can cause discrimination and produce suffering. We have also looked at the iatrogenic theory, that is, how medicine produces pathology (just think of healthcare bureaucracy or, again, medicalization): paradoxical, but true nonetheless.

Gregory Bateson, who is not usually counted among critical thinkers, provides the tools to overcome anthropocentrism and see humans as only a small part of the entire ecosystem and to understand that it is both foolish and arrogant to think that a single part (humans) can control the whole (the ecosystem). Bateson is, therefore, the bridge that connects OH to the social sciences. In particular, critical attention requires us to take account of different approaches to equity: environmental justice, interspecies justice, and intergenerational justice, in addition, of course, to social justice and intersectionality. The epistemic injustice approach is of particular importance. In general terms, epistemic injustice occurs as a failure to recognize the legitimacy of the knowledge held by a person or social group. Failure to recognize, Axel Honnett (1995) would say, is a form of violence. In the case of epistemic injustice, the failure to recognize a particular form of knowledge does not regard that knowledge in the strict sense, but rather those who possess it. We could call them the "transmitters," to use the jargon of the reassuring schematization of communication theory. They may be women, they may be indigenous peoples, they may be immigrants, they may be all of these. For this reason, such knowledge is ignored, disqualified, buried by other knowledge considered objective. It is, therefore, knowledge that is actively transformed into ignorance, as we saw in Chapter 3. Knowledge that will not flourish, will not develop, and will remain incomplete and unfinished (*undone science*). See Fig. 5.

There is clearly the risk of certain lay knowledge being confused with fake news or fabrications (from chemtrails to vaccines causing autism). This is why a certain degree of epistemic surveillance must be maintained, along with respect for traditional and lay knowledge.

One way to enhance lay knowledge and build consensus on OH policies is through social participation. This brings us to the second contribution of sociology.

Social participation is central to OH. The fields OH operates in are complex and turbulent: human, animal, and environmental health and all their

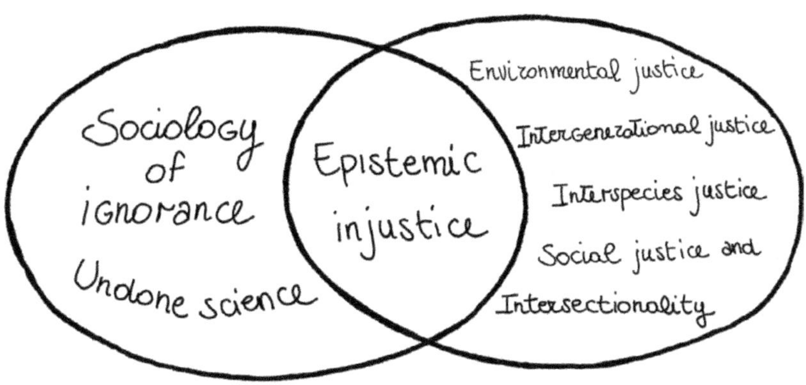

Fig. 5. Epistemic Injustice and Its Overlappings.

interconnections. These are areas where a top-down approach is doomed to failure. Community involvement is important for at least three reasons. First, in complex contexts, only "native" people or those with lay expertise can provide the fresh knowledge needed to design relevant interventions. Consequently, interventions often need to be co-produced in order to be effective, and this is the second reason. Third, in some cases, the people in a community are not only subjects of knowledge but also objects of the intervention, that is, they are the target. Their participation is essential to build consensus and legitimacy. Sociology, as we saw in Chapter 6, has developed numerous co-participation tools, ranging from living labs to creative methods (Moretti, 2023). In this way, we can attempt to engage stakeholders, expert citizens, and even indigenous populations, thus building a bridge between effectiveness and inclusiveness.

Let us now move on to the third point, which again regards methodology, but with a different aim. As we saw in Chapter 3, the OH approach can play a central role in predicting ecological and pandemic disasters. The focus on interdependence makes OH particularly suitable for picking up warning signals that may precede catastrophic events. Considering the dimension of interdependence results, in cognitive terms, results in the need for transdisciplinary thinking. This is a necessary orientation in a highly complex context in which parts interact in non-linear and unpredictable ways. It is also a scenario in which the future is not an extension of the past, which makes predictions difficult. Here, sociology can play a significant role. Sociology has solid methodological expertise that makes it central to future studies, and indeed, methodologies such as Delphi, Nominal Group Technique, scenario planning, and backcasting are established tools for social research in the field of forecasting.

I would now like to say something about the title of this last chapter. Although it is the final chapter, it is not definitive, hence the proposal for "unclusions" rather than conclusions. The first reason why this chapter is not definitive is that it does not put an end to the need to explore the sociological aspect of OH. Nor does the book as a whole, for that matter. My view is partial: having been socialized as a health sociologist, in this work, I have highlighted sociological aspects able to support the OH proposal. Most of these aspects are linked to health, although in this last chapter, I have proposed three concepts and three areas of work that I believe are sociological, broadly speaking.

Other sociologists, such as environmental sociologists, may see the role of sociology in OH in other ways. So now that we've come to the end of the work, I feel duty-bound to admit that this book is biased. It is a biased, non-definitive and unfinished text, but it humbly and clearly offers a take-home message regarding the role sociology can play in OH, and these last three areas of work are an invitation for colleagues to get involved.

NOTES

1. How companies learn your secrets, New York Times, 16 February 2012, available at https://www.nytimes.com/2012/02/19/magazine/shopping-habits.html (retrieved 30 November 2025).

2. How companies learn your secrets, New York Times, 16 February 2012, available at https://www.nytimes.com/2012/02/19/magazine/shopping-habits.html (retrieved 30 November 2025).

3. How Target Figured Out A Teen Girl Was Pregnant Before Her Father Did, Forbes, 16 February 2012, available at https://www.forbes.com/sites/kashmirhill/2012/02/16/how-target-figured-out-a-teen-girl-was-pregnant-before-her-father-did/ (retrieved 30 November 2025).

REFERENCES

American Public Health Association. (2019). *Public health code of ethics.* Retrieved from June 5, 2023, from https://www.apha.org/about-apha/apha-code-of-ethics

Arnold, K. E., Laing, G., McMahon, B. J., Fanning, S., Stekel, D. J., et al., McIntyre, J. M. (2024). The need for One Health systems-thinking approaches to understand multiscale dissemination of antimicrobial resistance. *Lancet Planet Health*, *8*(2), e124–e133. https://doi.org/10.1016/S2542-5196(23)00278-4

Christakis, N., & Fowler, J. (2009). *Connected. How your friends' friends' friends affect everything you feel, think and do.* Little, Brown and Co.

Conley, D., & Fletcher, J. (2017). *The genome factor: What the social genomics revolution reveals about ourselves, our history, and the future.* Princeton University Press.

Baquero, O. S. (2021). One Health of peripheries: Biopolitics, social determination, and field of praxis. *Frontiers in Public Health*, *30*(9). https://doi.org/10.3389/fpubh.2021.617003

Baquero, O. S., Benavidez Fernández, M. N., & Acero, A. M. (2021). From modern planetary health to decolonial promotion of One Health of peripheries. *Frontiers in Public Health*, *10*(9). https://doi.org/10.3389/fpubh.2021.637897

Beever, J., & Morar, N. (2017). Interconnectedness and interdependence: Challenges for public health ethics. *The American Journal of Bioethics*, *17*(9), 19–21. https://doi.org/10.1080/15265161.2017.1353175

Beever, J., & Morar, N. (2019). The epistemic and ethics onus of 'One Health'. *Bioethics*, *33*(1), 185–194. https://doi.org/10.1111/bioe.12522

Bossert, L. N. (2024). Interspecies justice within a normative sustainable development framework – Animal-friendly energy systems as a test case. *Journal of Agricultural and Environmental Ethics*, *37*(14). https://doi.org/10.1007/s10806-024-09933-1

Figueroa, J. F., Frakt, A. B., & Jha, A. (2020). Addressing social determinants of health: Time for a polysocial risk score. *Journal of American Medical Association*, *323*(16), 1553–1554. https://doi.org/10.1001/jama.2020.2436

Gao, P. (2021). The exposome in the era of One Health. *Environmental Science & Technology*, *55*(5), 2790–2799. https://doi.org/10.1021/acs.est.0c07033

Honnet, A. (1995). *The struggle for recognition*. Polity Press.

Ibanez, A., Melloni, L., Swiebopda, P., Hynes, W., Ikiz, B., et al., Eyre, H. A. (2024). Neuroecological links of the exposome and One Health. *Neuron*, *112*(12), 1905–1910. https://doi.org/10.1016/j.neuron.2024.04.016

Maturo, A. (2022). Polysocial risk scores and behavior-based health insurance: Promises and perils. *Tecnoscienza*, *13*(1), 106–115.

Maturo, A. (2024). *Il primo libro di sociologia della salute*. Einaudi.

Maturo, A., & Setiffi, F. (2023). *Wellness, social policy and public health: Bridging human flourishing with equity*. Emerald Publishing Limited.

Matus, P., Urquidi, C., Carcamo, M., & Vidal, V. (2024). Integrating the exposome and one health approach to national health surveillance: An opportunity for Latin American countries in health preventive management. *Frontiers in Public Health*, *12*, 1376609. https://doi.org/10.3389/fpubh.2024.1376609

McGinnis, J. M., Williams-Russo, P., & Knickman, J. R. (2002). The case for more active policy attention to health promotion. *Health Affairs*, *21*(2), 78–93. https://doi.org/10.1377/hlthaff.21.2.78

Meagher, K. M. (2024). Can One Health policy help us expand an ethics of interconnection and interdependence?. *AMA Journal of Ethics*, *26*(2), E162–E170. https://doi.org/10.1001/amajethics.2024.162

Moretti, V. (2023). *Understanding comics-based research: A practical guide for social scientists*. Emerald.

Nieuwland, J., & Meijboom, F. L. B. (2020). One Health: How interdependence enriches veterinary ethics education. *Animals*, *10*(13), 1–11. https://doi.org/10.3390/ani10010013

Rowe, R. (2021). Social determinants of health in the Big Data mode of population health risk calculation. *Big Data & Society*, *8*(2), 1–12. https://doi.org/10.1177/20539517211062881

Senier, L., Brown, P., Shostak, S., & Hanna, B. (2017). The socio-exposome: Advancing exposure science and environmental justice in a post-genomic era. *Environmental Sociology*, *3*(2), 107–121. https://doi.org/10.1080/23251042.2016.1220848

Swain, G. R., Burns, K. A., & Etkind, P. (2008). Preparedness: Medical ethics versus public health ethics. *Journal of Public Health Management and Practice*, *14*(4), 354–357. https://doi.org/10.1097/01.PHH.0000324563.87780.67

Van Patter, L., Linares-Roake, J., & Breen, A. V. (2023). What does One Health want? Feminist, posthuman, and anti-colonial possibilities. *One Health Outlook*, *5*(4), 1–9. https://doi.org/10.1186/s42522-022-00076-9

Wild, C. P. (2005). Complementing the genome with an "exposome": The outstanding challenge of environmental exposure measurement in molecular epidemiology. *Cancer Epidemiology, Biomarkers & Prevention*, *14*(8), 1847–1850. https://doi.org/10.1158/1055-9965.EPI-05-0456

INDEX

www.ingramcontent.com/pod-product-compliance
Lightning Source LLC
Chambersburg PA
CBHW072325210826
50226CB00039B/740